THE MEN:

American Enlisted Submariners in World War II; Why they joined, why they fought, and why they won.

by

Stephen Leal Jackson

First published by Dog Ear Publishing
4010 W. 86th Street, Ste H
Indianapolis, IN 46268
www.dogearpublishing.net

ISBN: 978-160844-487-8

This book is printed on acid-free paper.

Printed in the United States of America

To my wife, Sharon

Of course, submarines!

TABLE OF CONTENTS

ACKNOWLEDGEMENTS

FIRST, I EXTEND my appreciation and gratitude to all of the members of the Thames River Chapter of the United States Submarine Veterans of World War II in Groton, Connecticut, and especially to the men who consented to be interviewed for this project. Their openness, candor, and generosity allowed many important stories to be told and retold for the benefit of those of us who live in their debt. Several of these tales were related at the cost of some emotional pain as they recalled lost boats and absent companions. I was invited into their club meetings, into their homes, and into a personal and private part of their lives and am grateful for the friendship and courtesy these gentlemen showed me. I hope that I have done justice to their service and sacrifice.

Without the encouragement and support of my wife Sharon during the inception, development, and completion of this project, it could never have been completed. Her endless patience in the face of my seemingly endless requests only underscored the critical nature of a partner's help in such a long-term venture.

Ms. Wendy Gulley, archivist of the United States Navy Submarine Force Museum provided invaluable assistance in using the unique resource of the U.S. Navy submarine archives. The complete submarine war patrol reports were an important resource. During the very early days of my research, her introduction to the Harry F. Julian collection of letters helped provide focus and direction for the ultimate thesis of this book.

I also extend my thanks to the professors and staff of the Providence College History Department. Dr. Paul O'Malley was my mentor and guide in the development, research, and editing of this work. Dr. Thomas W. Grzebien III provided very useful comments that improved the clarity and flow of the book. Mrs. Phyllis Cardullo was a constant source of support, help, and encouragement throughout the entire project.

Mark H. Munro and Michael D. Brown were invaluable in providing technical advice and assistance in the final days of manuscript preparation. Their help with photograph scanning and image manipulation added significantly to the appearance of the book.

Finally, I can't forget my conscripted readers, Valerie K. Jackson, Linda A. Santoro, and Leslie L. Florio, who repaid my endless commentary, incessant prodding, and occasional artificial deadlines with a good-natured attitude and unflagging support.

LIST OF ILLUSTRATIONS

LIST OF ABBREVIATIONS

AS	Auxiliary Ship – Submarine Tender
ASR	Auxiliary Ship – Submarine Rescue
AVP	Auxiliary Ship – Aviation
BB	Battleship
CCC	Civilian Conservation Corps
CO	Commanding Officer
COB	Chief of the Boat
CPO	Chief Petty Officer
CS	Commissary Steward
CSC	Chief Commissary Steward
CSS	Confederate States Ship
DD	Destroyer
EM	Electrician's Mate
EMC	Chief Electrician's Mate
EN	Engineman
ENC	Chief Engineman
F	Fahrenheit
FM	Frequency Modulated (Sonar)
NAVPERS	Naval Personnel Manual
NELSCO	Diesel Engine Division of Electric Boat Shipyard
NUMA	National Underwater and Marine Agency
PC	Patrol Craft
POW	Prisoner of War
PSI	Pounds per Square Inch
QLA	Navy FM Scanning Sonar
RM	Radioman
RMC	Chief Radioman
R&R	Rest and Recreation
SFM	United States Navy Submarine Force Museum
SS	Ship - Submarine
SSN	Ship – Submarine – Nuclear
SSBN	Ship – Submarine – Ballistic Missile - Nuclear
SUBLANT	Commander, Submarine Forces – Atlantic Ocean

SUBPAC	Commander, Submarine Forces – Pacific Ocean
TDC	Torpedo Data Computer
TM	Torpedoman
TMC	Chief Torpedoman
USN	United States Navy
USS	United States Ship

FOREWORD

Jeweldeen "Deen" Brown
Connecticut State Commander,
United States Submarine Veterans of World War II

I FIRST MET Stephen Jackson in October, 2006. We discussed his objective, to write a book outlining the arduous life aboard submarines during World War II and to acknowledge the actions and accomplishments of the submarine enlisted crewmen. I was favorably impressed with his desire to illuminate this mostly undeveloped subject. His eight years of submarine service, combined with his extensive research of submarine operations, has provided him with a clear understanding of the vital performance of the submarine sailor. This subject has been largely neglected by authors, and especially the entertainment media, the latter often falsely portraying enlisted crewmen in movies in an uncomplimentary role; almost as pawns, acting only by officer direction. The wartime operation of a submarine in the "inner space" was a challenging matter, and every person on the crew was an independent expert. Knowledge of physics, engineering, earth topography, human physical limits, and life support all had to be learned, understood, and ever-present in thought and actions. These tenets were fundamental and were necessary to safely operate the vessel and to achieve its military mission objective, the delivery and deployment of weapons.

One noteworthy example of superb performance by an enlisted crewman is explained herein in the interview of Mr. Warren Wildes. There an enlisted man, using his training, experience, and skill, successfully guided the USS *Flying Fish* through a previously impervious enemy minefield in order to safely enter and exit the Sea of Japan.

For myself, an enlisted man and submarine combat veteran during World War II, it was refreshing to have a historian research this subject, which has received so little attention. Sub Vet Jackson was clearly able to understand the experiences and challenges of life on an undersea warship even though his service occurred long after World

War II had ended.   As the Connecticut State Commander, United States Submarine Veterans of World War II, I consider it both my duty and my pleasure to commend Stephen Jackson for his thoroughly researched, accurately written, and enjoyable to read book.   He has helped animate the courage and volunteer character that made the "Silent Service" the elite fighting force of World War II.   This spirit, thus born, remains alive and vibrant in the submarine force today.

J. B., October, 2009

When discussing vessels of the United States Navy, it is typical to describe the crew in the terms, "...the officers and the men...," as RADM Arleigh Burke, USN, did in his December 1950 study, *Discipline in the U.S. Navy.*

The majority of the books written about submarine activities during World War II focused on the actions of the officers.

This book, however, was written about the men.

USS *Sturgeon* (SS 187) and crew at New London, CT, c. January 1945.
Courtesy SFM

CHAPTER 1

INTRODUCTION

Lord God, our power evermore,
Whose arm doth reach the ocean floor,
Dive with our men beneath the sea;
Traverse the depths protectively.
O hear us when we pray, and keep
Them safe from peril in the deep.

David B. Miller,
Eternal Father, Strong to Save – Submariner's Verse

Preface

THE JAPANESE ATTACK on Pearl Harbor and the subsequent declaration of a state of war by Germany galvanized the patriotic fervor of the American people. While many young men wanted to serve their country in its time of need, they also wanted to find a place where they could serve productively, maybe experience some adventure and some glory, and hopefully emerge safely from the experience. Considering this, a seemingly unlikely choice was service in the American Submarine Force during World War II. Duty on submarines was one of the most dangerous, arduous, and emotionally challenging assignments in the U.S. Navy. The boats, as they were called, were Spartan in the area of creature comforts, and a war patrol, typically thirty to sixty days in length, was so exhausting it required the submarine sailors to take up to a full month of rest and relaxation, R&R, on their return. However, the navy did not have to institute conscription until the end of 1942, and the Submarine Service never had any difficulty in acquiring quality volunteers.[1] Those volunteers who

1

possessed the needed skills and could physically qualify fought their way onto the submarines by persistence, influence, and occasionally guile.

What would motivate men to preferentially seek out what may have been the most dangerous branch of the service? By the end of the war over 3,500 submariners, over to 23 percent of the force, never returned from their missions; fifty-two World War II submarines are "still on patrol."[2] The enlisted men, upon whom this research focuses, had even fewer apparent benefits from this choice of military service. But they sought out a place on the boats out of desire to perform a meaningful, useful, military task in a front-line position where there was a very high likelihood that if they came back, they would come back a whole man. This presupposes some affinity for submarines that came from either a natural attraction to the craft, familiarity through working on or near them, or some positive experience through the direct contact with or recommendation of a mentor. The potential sub sailor could not be too fond of the formality of the "spit-and-polish" navy, since submarines are relatively informal places, especially with regard to those navy traditions that are more form than substance.

The role of the enlisted, non-officer submariner has been largely ignored by both scholarly and historical fiction writers, who have instead concentrated on the submarine's Captain and other officers' motivations, actions, and opinions as an embodiment of the institution of the submarine on war patrol. The enlisted men, with few exceptions, were relegated to the role of minor players, and their experiences, their feelings, and their contributions were, for the most part, unexamined. This may have occurred without design because the post-war submarine writers of submarine stories were, for the most part, ex-commanding officers. In addition, due to the closeness of living and working conditions and the intense situations of warfare that the men experienced, the crew and the submarine tended to weld themselves into a single cohesive unit where the successes, failures, and experiences are shared and owned by the unit. However, the choice of the enlisted man to descend into the submarine at war was that much more extraordinary considering the relative anonymity in which he performed.

The methodology for the research of this book was to build a foundation of primary source information derived from interviews conducted with enlisted submarine veterans of World War II.

Through presentations at meetings of the Thames Chapter of the Submarine Veterans of World War II, I was able to make connections with many men willing to talk about their wartime experiences. I was privileged to be able to conduct personal, extensive interviews with such men. The life they were able to breathe into the static facts of the time period enriched and illuminated this project and provided enlightening firsthand accounts of some of the iconic military events of World War II. Although there was reluctance among some veterans about discussing their experiences, I was fortunate in the variety of navy occupations, diversity in ages, and uniqueness of experiences in my interviews. In addition to these interviews, support for my book was derived exclusively from primary sources, including collections of letters, official government war patrol reports, and books written exclusively by enlisted submarine sailors. Areas of incidental support and background information, when they are not supported by these primary sources, depend on universally accepted reference authorities such as *Jane's Fighting Ships*, United States Navy websites and other scholarly sources. The Submarine Force Museum, located adjacent to the United States Naval Submarine Base in Groton, Connecticut, is the repository for a vast collection of submarine war reports, scrapbooks, letters, diaries, and published materials concerning the role of the submariner, and it was an unparalleled asset for this type of research.

As an eight-year veteran of the United States Submarine Service, I served on two boats. One of these boats made extensive patrols in the Pacific and Indian Ocean regions, which was also the area of primary interest in the World War II submarine conflict. Because of this experience, I was able to establish an instant rapport with the interviewees and forego the need for time-consuming explanations about topics every submariner naturally understands. For example, a sub sailor, whether he served on a World War II fleet boat or a modern nuclear fast attack, has experienced the complex procedures, frustrating failures, and occasional hilarious disasters involved with the humble task of "flushing" the toilet. As a former submarine sailor, I also feel that I was the beneficiary of the high level of pride and professionalism of America's naval submarine force that was made possible by the efforts and sacrifices of these extraordinary men.

CHAPTER 2

THE LIFE SUBMARINE

Prepare, prepare the iron helm of war,
Bring forth the lots, cast in the spacious orb;
Th' Angel of Fate turns them with mighty hands,
And casts them out upon the darken'd earth!
Prepare, prepare!

William Blake,
A War Song to Englishmen

Introduction

TO UNDERSTAND THE men who chose to descend into the dangerous depths in tiny, fragile boats, it is necessary to understand a bit of the technology, design, and inherent hazards of the World War II-era American submarine. The birth and development of the sub-surface warship, often a child of necessity, is a tale of adventure and curiosity and occasionally desperation. Man has always yearned to experience the freedom of the skies and delve into the mysteries of the seas. Of these two alien elements, the sea is the least forgiving. Trips into the sky are taken with the knowledge that whether the flight is successful or a failure, it will ultimately end on the ground, albeit sometimes more quickly than is beneficial. Not so with underwater trips, where the first foot of descent begins the pressure increase that will inevitably crush even the stoutest vessel. At sea level, atmospheric pressure is about 14.7 pounds per square inch (PSI). At thirty-three feet below sea level, this pressure approximately doubles, and another atmosphere of pressure is added for every additional thirty-two feet of descent.[1] At three hundred feet below sea level, the depth often sought by American World War II fleet submarines under surface attack, the pressure on the hull of a submarine would be about 150 PSI. At this level, the pressure seeks out the weakest point of the vessel, so depth charges did not need to destroy huge parts of a submarine but only had to create or weaken a vulnerable component to provide access to the killing pressure and the pressing seas.

Alexander the Great, the most notable of ancient submariners, was reputed to have descended into the Adriatic Sea c.330 BC contained in a "bell" filled with air for a brief journey below the surface.[2] As undersea vessels were improved from the crude diving bell until the beginning of the twentieth century, breathing air was carried in submarines almost incidentally and consisted of what could be held within the confines of the vessel. Between Alexander's legendary trip and the 1940s, many experiments were conducted with submarine technology, both for exploratory and military purposes.

A young American, David Bushnell, a student at Yale and a contemporary of Nathan Hale, developed the first functioning submarine in 1775. The ungainly barrel-shaped craft was propelled by the power of its lone crewman and could dive, maneuver, and return to the surface. Named the *Turtle*, this crude submarine was used in July, 1776, to attack the HMS *Eagle*, the flagship of the British fleet blockading New York harbor. Bushnell's attempt to attach a black-powder explosive charge on the hull of the *Eagle* was unsuccessful, though his submarine did escape and did survive the counterattack.[3]

The opening act of successful submarine warfare began with the sinking of the Union sloop-of-war USS *Housatonic* by the Confederate submarine CSS *Horace L. Hunley* on February 17, 1864, during the American Civil War. In addition to being the first submarine to sink another vessel in combat, the crude but effective *Hunley* contained many features that, though rudimentary in their form, were not seen again until the advent of the World War II-era submarine designs. The *Hunley* contained innovative features such as diving planes to control depth, pumps to manage water ballast, a single propeller and rudder, and internal ballast tanks. Since electrical storage batteries were not available, the *Hunley* used eight men on a propulsion crankshaft to provide motive force. Her weapon was a spar-mounted torpedo jutting out from the bow that was driven into the hull of her intended victim. Although the *Hunley* was claustrophobically sized and had the dubious distinction of killing her first two training crews, including her inventor, the Confederates had no trouble recruiting another crew for her first and final combat mission.[4] While the exact motivations of the *Hunley's* daring crews are unknown, twenty-two of her crew members gave their lives serving onboard this new technology. Although the submarine's tangible impact on the Union fleet was small, the knowledge that the Confederates possessed these stealthy and effective craft proved to be a "powerful psychological warfare tool"[5] that slowed Union control of southern ports and caused extensive defensive security changes, which allowed more successful blockade running by Confederates. A submarine would not again sink a ship in combat until 1914, when the Imperial German submarine *U-21* sank the British cruiser *Pathfinder*.[6]

The Modern Naval Submarine

The history of modern submarine warfare in America began on April 4, 1900, with the United States Navy's acceptance of John Phillip Holland's submarine, the USS *Holland* (SS 1).[7] The Navy's first commissioned submarine, the *Holland* was also the first functional submarine in the world to be employed in a non-experimental role. Though microscopic compared to the underwater boats that were soon to follow, the *Holland* had all of the key aspects that are indicative of the effective modern submarine. Her dual propulsion system used a gasoline engine for surface operation and battery charging and batteries for submerged travel. This combination, except for the replacement of gasoline fuel with diesel, was the pattern for almost all submarines to follow until the advent of naval nuclear propulsion in the 1950s. A fixed center of gravity and an improved ballasting system allowed for stability on the surface and while submerged, while the hydrodynamic shape made this craft a true undersea vessel. The final modern aspect was the weapon system, primarily the tube-launched torpedo, which allowed the submarine to strike from a distance and a position of stealth and then to slip away.

The *Holland* boats were functional but crude; truly a modern military warship but with more in common with the Model T Ford than with the more sophisticated surface war vessels of the time. They were powered by what amounted to an automobile engine that leaked enough exhaust into the boat as to endanger the crew. The

USS *Holland* (SS 1), c. 1900.
Courtesy SFM

humble remedy to this was to take a lesson from the old coal miners and bring onboard a "living" early warning system: mice. Suspended in a cage near the engine, the crew watched their condition; as long as these tiny passengers were "frisky," all was well. When the mice became asphyxiated, the Captain knew it was time to secure the engine and send the human crew topside.[8] From the birth of these tiny, fragile craft, the someday large and powerful family of the American Navy submarine had been founded.

Like the USS *Holland*, the first American submarines were given names. Beginning a tradition that would last until the 1970s, submarines were named after fish. Though the more pugilistic names such as *Shark*, *Stingray*, and *Pike* were early favorites, there are only so many angry fish, so eventually the more benign *Chub*, *Tuna*, and *Cod* donated their names to the fleet. But bold or tame, the naming of submarines was a short-lived tradition in America. Around 1914 the navy began naming submarines with a letter and number designation. For example, the seventh submarine in the first group of submarines delivered by John Holland was renamed from its original USS *Shark* to USS *A-7*.[9] This apparent loss of distinction actually brought the vessels more in line with the convention for the naming of ships in the U.S. Navy. In short, only important fleet vessels were given class-defining names, while service craft received just letters and numbers.

The initial conception of the submarine's mission was simply as a coastal or harbor defense ship. Early limitations in speed, range, weaponry, and crew support features made it impossible for these boats to travel with the fleet. For missions in remote areas, the early subs would always be chaperoned by a support craft; this vessel was called a submarine tender. The transition from coastal defender to fleet boat was gradual, and each succeeding class included improvements and experiments as the technology evolved. A true fleet-worthy submarine, or fleet boat, would have to be able to travel at greater than seventeen knots, deploy effective weapons, and have a cruising range of greater than 6,000 nautical miles mainly to keep up with the battleships. These ships were the flagships or leaders of naval battle groups and set the pace for all of the ships in their command. For example, the USS *New Mexico* (BB 40), built in 1914 but extensively remodeled in the 1930s, could travel at speeds up to 21 knots and had a cruising range of 6,000 nautical miles at a speed of 12 knots.[10]

Table 1 shows the evolution of the American submarine classes from the initial tiny Holland to the all-purpose fleet boat. Note the incremental increases in speed, range, depth, and weapons capabilities. Also of note, but not shown on the table, the number of members of each class tended to increase as the technology approached the ideal configuration. Due to the rapid improvement in the technology and incorporation of lessons learned into the subsequent class, the early classes of submarines contained very few members. However, the impetus of World War I and a relative stabilization of the technology allowed the O-class to grow to sixteen boats, and the R-class grew to twenty-seven.[11]

Table 1: The Evolving Capabilities for the Developing American Submarine Classes[i]

Sub Class	Date of First Issue	Displace (sub. tons)	Length (feet)	Speed (surf. knots)	Range (n. miles)	Depth (feet)	Crew	Torpedo Tubes / Load
Holland	1900	64	54'10"	5	n/a	100	7	1 / 3
A	1903	123	63'10"	8	n/a	150	7	1 / 3
B	1907	173	82'6"	9	n/a	150	10	2 / 4
C	1908	275	105'4"	10	n/a	200	15	2 / 4
D - N								
O	1918	629	172'	14	5000	200	29	4 / 8
R	1918	598	186'	12	3700	200	29	4 / 8
S: 1,18-41	1918	1062	219'	15	5000	200	42	4 / 12
S: 3-17	1918	1092	231'	15	5000	200	42	5 / 14
S: 42-47	1918	1126	216'	15	8000	200	42	4 / 12
S: 48-51	1918	1230	240'	14.5	8000	200	42	4 / 12
AA-1 / T	1920	1107	268'	20	3000	150	55	6 / 16
Barracuda	1921	2620	341'	18	12000	250	80	6 / 12
Porpoise	1935	1934	301'	19	10000	250	50	6 / 16
Salmon	1938	2198	308'	21	9500	250	70	8 / 24
Sargo	1939	2350	310'	21	9500	250	70	8 / 24
Tambor	1940	2370	307'	20	9500	250	80	10 / 24
Gato	1940	2424	311'	21	11000	300	60	10 / 24
Balao	1943	2424	311'	20	11800	400	80	10 / 24
Tench	1944	2428	307'	20	12000	300	80	10 / 24

Note: Statistics are typical for member boats of the described submarine classes. Classes not detailed are either small issue, experimental classes, or do not materially contribute to the ultimate development of either the Fleet Submarines or the "S"-Boats. Classes D through N, specifically, exemplified this rapid technology.

---

[i] Note: Information in the Appendix compiled from the following sources: *Jane's Fighting Ships of WW II.* London: Studio Editions Ltd., 1989. Originally published by Jane's Publishing Co. 1946/47; Hoyt, Edwin P. *Submarines At War: The History of the American Silent Service.* Brancliff Manor, NY: Stein and Day, 1983.; Bagnasco, Erminio, ed. *Submarines of World War Two.* Annapolis, Maryland, Naval Institute Press, 1977.

The S-Class Boats

The art of manufacturing the best littoral or coastal defense submarine reached its apex with the S-class submarine. The S-boats, sometimes nicknamed 'Sugar" boats, were perfectly designed for short to medium forays from a harbor or support craft. But due to still-limited armament, speed, and range, they could not easily travel with the fleet. These submarines fully incorporated all of the lessons learned from reverse engineering the Imperial German *Untersee* (U) boats gained as war prizes in the Great War. As such, they were a vast improvement over the previous American submarine types, and though they spanned the roles of submarine as coastal defender to submarine as fleet cruiser, they still left much to be desired. S-boats, except for the last few constructed, did not have air conditioning, which though primarily provided to maintain environmental conditions for electronics and machinery, also somewhat mitigated the awful heat and humidity that the sailor had to endure. If a boat ran its diesel engines all night to charge batteries, when the boat submerged at dawn and shut down the engines, the heat from their operation would be trapped inside the boat. After such a run, temperatures in the engine room would routinely exceed 120° F.[12]

The S-boats had several different configurations but generally had four torpedo tubes in the forward part of the boat and a weapons load of twelve torpedoes. Their lack of air conditioning, very limited ability to make fresh water, and sparse crew comfort accommodations led to their gaining the well-deserved nickname of "pigboats." Especially in the tropics, the inability to control the interior environment created conditions of high temperature and humidity that were often debilitating to the men and hard on the machinery. The crew, typically six officers and forty-five men, all had to share bunks. A single washbasin held about a pint of water that a man could use to brush his teeth or wash his face. Occasionally, the torpedo alcohol fuel was used as a cleanser for a sponge bath. In a war zone, the S-boat's heads, or toilets, would be secured, requiring the crew to make use of the bilges and buckets that would ultimately have to be passed through the mess hall before being emptied topside.[13]

The moist, hot conditions allowed "stowaway" insects and occasionally rats to flourish, while skin sores and rashes were

USS *S-48* (SS 159), c. 1930.
Courtesy SFM

commonplace in the human occupants. Clothing and footwear, when worn, would disintegrate under these conditions. All of these routine hardships were made worse when the S-boats were pushed beyond their capabilities to meet the necessities of war in the crisis days after December 7, 1941. Of the one hundred and eleven submarines in commission when the United States declared war on the Empire of Japan only thirty-eight were the more modern fleet-type submarines. [14]

The remainder were mainly the older S-boats, and these World War I vintage submarines were called upon to hold back the tide of the advancing enemy even though they were assessed to be "too slow, short-legged, and fragile for extended operations with the fleet."[15] Surprisingly though, the S-boats, through the skill and determination of their crews, amassed a creditable record of sinkings, special missions, and general fleet support. Certainly aware of the limitations of the submarine fleet at the commencement of the war, Admiral Chester W. Nimitz, commander of naval forces in the Pacific, praised these ships and these men when he said, "During the dark, early months of World War II, it was only the tiny American submarine force that held off the Japanese Empire and enabled our fleets to replace their losses and repair their wounds. The spirit and courage of the Submarine Force shall never be forgotten."[16]

The American Fleet-Type Submarine

USS *Becuna* (SS 319), c. 1944.
Courtesy SFM

The fleet submarine, or fleet boat, was a compact little home away from home, with the emphasis on compact. At the onset of World War II, the technology, if not the requisite numbers of boats, had been developed. During World War II, the *Gato* and the *Balao* classes of submarines embodied the best attributes of this boat style and were constructed in the greatest number, counting over two hundred members by war's end.[17] Five shipyards were responsible for constructing theses new classes of fleet submarines. These were Electric Boat Company in Groton, Connecticut; Portsmouth Naval Shipyard in Kittery, Maine; Mare Island Naval Shipyard in Vallejo, California; Manitowoc Shipbuilding in Manitowoc, Wisconsin; and Cramp Shipbuilding in Philadelphia, Pennsylvania. These true fleet boats could achieve speeds of greater than twenty knots per hour on the surface and nine knots per hour submerged, had a range of greater than 11,000 nautical miles, were equipped with six torpedo tubes forward and four aft, carried a wartime load of twenty-four torpedoes, were propelled by four diesel-electric drive engines, contained watertight compartments, could achieve a maximum depth of between 300 and 400 feet, and were manned by a crew of sixty to eighty five men.[18]

The transition to the higher level of technology began with the construction of the *Barracuda* class, the first class to be deliberately designed to operate with the fleet. These attributes were developed more completely in the *Porpoise* class and were fulfilled in the *Tambor* class; this was the definitive fleet-type submarine (see Table 1). The 1939 printing of *The Bluejacket's Manual*, a handbook for the American recruit sailor, described the status of the United States submarine fleet. "Our larger submarines (Barracuda type) are designed to accompany the fleet on extended cruises, and have quite a long cruising radius. The other submarines have a maximum of about 14 knots speed and are designed primarily to operate from bases."[19] In addition, faster speeds, deeper diving capability, increased and improved crew accommodations, air conditioning, and just lots more space were some of the technological improvements made in this new class. The *Porpoise* class was also the first to be fabricated using all welded construction, greatly improving their strength and battle endurance. It also was the first to employ all-electric drive, where the four main engines produced only electricity, not motive force, which was then used to power the drive motors and to charge the storage batteries.[20]

George Jones, one of the veterans whose experiences will be related later in this book, served both on S-class and fleet boats during the war and worked at Electric Boat shipyard in Groton, Connecticut, after retiring from the navy. He commented on just how much improved the fleet submarines were compared to their World War I vintage S-boat cousins.

> After I went to EB and being in the Design Department I saw all the plans for the nuclear boats available at that time and I used to say it would be no more revolutionary to go from a fleet boat to a nuclear boat than going from an S-boat to a fleet boat.[21]

Duty on the fleet boats was sought after, especially when the choice was one of these newer submarines or one of the older S-boats. Almost every sailor would choose the fleet boat, and in situations where volunteers could not be found, out came the "straws." Another World War II submarine veteran, John Deane, was in the quartermaster rating, responsible for assisting in navigation and signaling. He was on R&R between war patrols when a request came in from two submarines needing a man with his rating specialty, the fleet boat USS *Seawolf* (SS 197) and the USS *S-47* (SS 158), built in 1921. Deane remembered losing the contest.

> And there were three of us (quartermasters) in the relief crew and none of us wanted that S-boat. I mean, that was — that boat was older than I was. Actually it was six months older than I was. So, anyways, I drew the short straw and I got the S-boat. I've got to admit I moaned and groaned a bit about getting that boat, rotten deal and so forth. Six weeks later I got word that the quartermaster that got on the *Seawolf* was gone. It went down. I considered myself very fortunate and I never bitched again.[22]

Deane was certainly relieved that he had been spared by the pull of a straw, but compared to the fleet boats, he agreed that the S-boats were definitely "rugged duty."

The American fleet-type submarine had evolved into the perfect weapon to serve the needs of the wartime commanders. But how did it serve the needs of its crew during the war patrols, often lasting more than sixty days? The degree of privation experienced during these war patrols was evidenced by the routine practice of allowing the crew up to a month of relaxation after a grueling patrol in specially designated rest camps where relaxing, sunbathing, beer-drinking, and ball-playing were the order of the day. The fleet boat was a tool; it

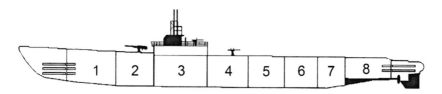

Fleet boat compartments cross-section:
1. Forward torpedo room, 2. Forward battery compartment,
3. Control room (Conning tower above), 4. After battery compartment,
5. Forward engine room, 6. After engine room, 7. Maneuvering room,
8. After torpedo room.
Graphic by the author

was a machine of war where crew comforts, when they existed at all, were subordinate or an adjunct to the military use.

The fleet submarine was divided into discrete, watertight compartments, each with a primary purpose but each also functioning as a multi-purpose space. [23] Starting at the bow of the sub, the forward torpedo room, about thirty feet from the tubes to the after hatch and sixteen feet across, was a good example of this dual usage principle. Obviously, the torpedo room's primary function was to store, prepare, and launch these weapons as efficiently as possible. To accomplish this task, the *Gato* class submarine had six torpedo tubes in this forward room and sixteen torpedoes; six were in the tubes ready to be fired, and ten were on storage racks available for reload. In this 480 square feet of space were also jammed the officer's head, various support machinery, and bunks and lockers for at least ten crewmen.[24] These ten bunks were often efficiently used by a procedure known as "hot racking." When the total number of available bunks, or beds, exceeded the number of crew, two men, on different shifts or watches, would share a bunk. Ideally, when a submariner was ready for some rest, his bunkmate would just be rising, allowing him to jump into the still "hot" rack. The cozy bunks in this torpedo room were placed adjacent to or directly on top of the live torpedoes resting in their own torpedo racks. Whether it was the companionship of a neighboring Mark XIV torpedo, or the regular shift of men working in the torpedo room, a sailor with a bunk in this space was never lonely. Additionally, the forward torpedo room, being one of the larger spaces, often doubled as the movie theater and community room, especially for church services.[25]

Directly aft of the forward torpedo room was the forward battery compartment, home to the Captain's stateroom, the wardroom where the officers dined, the officers' and Chief Petty Officer's quarters, the officers' shower, and the office of the Yeoman, or Ship's Clerk. Rather than being isolated in perfect splendor, the fleet boat officer's "country" was routinely invaded by a stream of enlisted crew who lived, worked, and relaxed in the forward torpedo room. The officers also had the distinction of living just above one hundred and twenty six storage batteries; these comprised the forward battery bank.

Moving toward the stern, a crewman would next pass through the nerve center of the boat, the control room. Herein resided most of the electrical circuits and switchboards, air manifolds and controls, diving and navigational controls, and the radio room. Beneath the control room was the pump room containing equipment for moving and removing water, compressing air, the air conditioning and refrigeration machines, and the trim pump. Where a drain pump would be used to remove large quantities of water from the sub, the trim pump moved water back and forth to trim tanks to balance the buoyancy of the boat so that when it dove it reached its desired depth in a relatively "level" condition.[26] Above the control room was the conning tower, the brain to the control room's nervous system. Here all of the navigational decisions, fire control solutions, and command and control orders were initiated. Within the conning tower were the periscopes, used for visual sightings and directional data acquisition, and the torpedo data computer (TDC), which generated torpedo firing solutions based on information about target speed, distance, and angle relative to the submarine. Once these solutions, including depth and heading for the torpedoes to follow, were calculated, the torpedoes were guided by their own internal gyrocompasses.[27]

Directly aft of the control room was a different kind of nerve center, the center of the enlisted crew's activities. The after battery compartment housed the galley, the mess deck, and crew's berthing. The galley was responsible for producing four meals a day for about eighty men and was incredibly small but contained all the basics: ovens, deep fryers, griddle, mixer, and the ubiquitous giant coffee urn. An article in *LIFE* magazine in 1943 described the galley as "...less than a third the size of a Pullman dining car" and stated that the Cook could touch all four walls without moving.[28] Key to the morale of the crew, the Cook, and especially the baker, used their limited space and often unlimited talents to create plentiful, quality meals, given the challenges of the situation. Martin Sheridan, a reporter who joined the USS *Bullhead* on one of her war patrols, succinctly captured the importance of food in his book, *Overdue and Presumed Lost*. "A good baker and a good Cook are two important requisites toward achieving a happy submarine crew. Next to resting in the sack, eating is the greatest pastime on these crowded craft. Maybe eating is the more important."[29]

On the mess deck, four tables, two feet by five feet, could serve twenty-four men at one sitting. The padded bench seats doubled as storage and were adequate seating, but the backrest was either the bulkhead or the man behind. When meals were not being served, this one hundred and eight square foot space, about the size of a small bedroom, was used by the crew for leisure time activities such as letter writing, card playing, clothing maintenance, or "shooting-the-bull."[30]

The crew's berthing area, aft of the mess deck, contained thirty-six racks and lockers for the balance of the enlisted men. Again, hot racking was common, even in this larger dormitory, and they were arranged by rank. An experienced first class petty officer might get his very own bunk, while a new seaman second class would most likely have to share. All of these spaces in this compartment were on the deck above the after battery bank and the ammunition locker. The batteries and the crew had a love/hate relationship. The crew loved the batteries, since they provided the boat's power while submerged and, after the boat sustained a virulent depth charge attack, were the motive force to return to the surface. They hated them because they consumed the lion's share of the fresh water on board and, if they were cracked during an attack, had the dangerous capacity for generating chlorine gas from the sulfuric acid and seawater mixture.[31]

Moving aft, the next two compartments were the forward and the after engine rooms. Each watertight compartment contained two large diesel engines, like the General Motors Model 16-248 V16 diesel engines on the USS *Gato* (SS 212), that directly drove an electric generator, sending its electrical output either to one of the electric drive motors that propelled the ship or to charge the battery. On the *Gato* class subs, all four engines combined generated a total of 5,400 horsepower for main propulsion on the surface. A much smaller engine, called the "dinky," located in the lower level of the after engine room, was used in extreme emergencies to charge batteries or provide direct propulsion. Since the field of the generator of the "dinky" was self-exciting, it required no external electrical connection to start the generator field to begin generating electricity; the dinky could assist in the re-start of the main diesel engines if no battery power was available. Also, in cases where submarines found themselves very low on fuel, it was possible to use the more frugal dinky to provide propulsion, albeit very slowly and only on the surface.[32]

Almost at the stern of the boat, the maneuvering room was the next compartment located aft of the engine rooms. The maneuvering station, a panel of electrical controls, allowed the Electrician's Mates on watch to take engine orders from the control room. This station had the ability to control the speed and direction of both propellers and to line up the output of the diesel-driven electric generators to the battery or to the electric motors attached to one of the two reduction gears. On the same level as the maneuvering control station were the remote controls for diesel engine shutdown, a lathe for fabrication of repair parts, and the crew's head. Below this level was the motor room containing four main motors, two for each reduction gear / propeller shaft assembly, and associated cooling and lubricating oil pumps.

Finally, at the stern of the boat, was the after torpedo room. Unlike its forward counterpart, this room had only four torpedo tubes, loaded with four torpedoes. Four spare torpedoes for reload were on racks alongside the compartment. Similar to the forward room, the after torpedo room was also used for crew berthing, and using stern tubes in the after torpedo room was more of a morale-building event than could be attributed to the satisfaction of sinking of enemy shipping. In his book *Thunder Below!*, Admiral Fluckey, onetime Captain of the fleet boat USS *Barb*, related a report from the officer in charge of the after torpedo room. "Captain, reload complete. My men want to thank you for using the stern tubes. It's the first time on a *Barb* patrol. We've already turned the three empty torpedo skids into nine bunks. Please shoot one more from aft, then everyone will have a bunk of their own."[33] Due to the extreme distance between these two torpedo rooms, but the identical occupations of their inhabitants, lively competitions would often spring up between them, with ships sunk, torpedoes expended, and shiniest torpedo tube doors among the measures of success.[34]

The Men

The men who made up a typical crew of a fleet submarine came from a number of different navy backgrounds. At the beginning of the war, many were Asiatic Fleet veterans, experienced and hardened by long service in the older, more primitive boats. Their knowledge would be used later to train the new recruits in the Submarine School and on the boats. Also, these submariners were familiar with the environment that would be the location for war patrols, the Pacific and Indian Oceans, and the challenges and difficulties the men would face in those areas. At the onset of hostilities, it was still a stated navy policy to require at least a year of surface navy experience before a sailor could volunteer for the submarine service, but the exigencies of war caused this requirement to be often ignored and eventually abandoned early in the conflict. Men could then be inducted directly into the boats, but only after passing a rigorous physical exam, completing their service (trade) school, and making it through Submarine School. Only about one out of every ten applicants made it to serve on the boats.[35] In March 1942, *LIFE* magazine accurately described the students at the U.S. Navy's Submarine School at New London, Connecticut. "The students are all volunteers and there is always a waiting list. For submarine service is a coveted duty, given only to men who are suited to its hardships."[36] On relatively rare occasions, a sailor could be assigned to a submarine without going through Submarine School.

Approximately fifty to sixty men comprised a sub's enlisted crew. Divided into specialized departments, they were led by their Chief Petty Officers (CPO), a senior enlisted man who was well qualified and experienced in his job and in submarine operations. The departments the CPOs supervised contained different ratings for all of the tasks that needed to be performed onboard. The Weapons department would have Torpedomen to maintain and launch the "fish" (torpedoes) and Gunner's Mates to take care of the deck guns and smaller weapons. Enginemen or Motor Machinist's Mates would operate the diesel engines and also perform repairs on all mechanical equipment. The Electrician's Mates stood watch at the maneuvering station and maintained all electrical equipment aboard. At the beginning of the era of electronics, the Radioman was responsible for all of the new technology, like radar, in addition to performing his radio communications duties. Quartermasters helped navigate the boat, the Yeoman was the ship's clerk, and the Cooks and Bakers provided around-the-clock meals and baked goods, greatly appreciated by all hands.[37]

The enlisted crew as a whole was led by the Chief of the Boat (COB). This man could be from any rating but was always the senior enlisted man. Often called just "The COB," he was the crew's direct representative to the Captain and also acted as the liaison for orders and directions that affected all departments. At his best, the COB was a stern but loving uncle; he was approachable and would encourage new men with their assimilation to the crew, but he was equally as able to enforce established standards and swiftly correct those who deviated from them.[38]

It seems reasonable to assume that men who grew up and lived near the oceans would have a greater affinity for choosing navy service than those men who lived far from the sea ,but that appears not necessarily to have been the case. The state of mass communications in the 1930s and 1940s was advanced enough in the United States to provide almost everyone with exposure to the possibilities of a naval career; the most effective means of accomplishing this seems to have been through the motion pictures. Movies showed the glamour, the heroism, and the glory of the navy, accentuating the positives as only this medium could. The men who were attracted by this means were usually drawn to the battleships since, as the navy's primary weapon afloat before the war, they gave the appearance of affording the highest potential for adventure and glory. The only men who were drawn directly to the submarines were generally those who lived near or worked in a submarine manufacturing shipyard or had a member of their family already in the submarine service. Not until the war actually began were movies produced, like *Destination Tokyo*, that depicted the submarine also as a glamorous war machine.[39]

Qualification in Submarines

While a sailor's tenure at Submarine School gave him the basic knowledge of the design and operation of these craft, every man was expected to qualify on his boat within about six months after reporting onboard. For the 1940s sub sailor, qualification meant understanding all of the systems onboard the boat and generally knowing how to do most everyone's job. For example, an Electrician would be expected to know how to start one of the diesel engines, to line up air systems to blow ballast tanks, and to fire a torpedo. He certainly would not be as fast or as skilled as a Torpedoman, but the qualified submariner could be considered a competent and interchangeable crew member for most critical positions in the event of some catastrophic emergency. *The Bluejacket's Manual*, the recruit handbook, made this very clear to those seeking a career in submarines:

> To qualify as a submarine man, certain requirements must be fulfilled. He must have served at least six months on submarines. Before presenting himself for examination, the candidate must submit a notebook. The book must contain all data specified by "Submarine Instructions." The examination is an oral and practical one. It consists in going through the boat and operating all apparatus in the boat and answering any questions pertaining to the same. A commissioned officer conducts the examination.[40]

This notebook contained drawings done by the candidate of all of the ship's systems, including important settings, volumes, and setpoints. Information in the notebook was the focus of the examination, but not the sum of what could be asked. Qualification meant being able to remain on the boat. Sailors unable to qualify were transferred, often to a tender or relief crew. For those who made it, there came initiation as a real submarine crew member, the ability to develop and advance in his rating, and that little embroidered patch on his right sleeve halfway between the wrist and elbow that told the world, "This is a submarine sailor."[41]

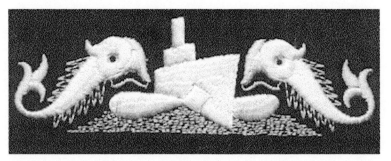

Submarine qualification badge "Dolphins" on dress blue cloth.
From author's collection

Being a qualified submarine sailor had monetary advantages as well. Recognizing the danger of even routine submarine operations, the crew was paid a premium while serving on one of the boats. This could boost their pay by 50 percent, depending on their rank and rating.[42]

The Captain

A former fleet boat Captain accurately described how a Captain's personality was infused throughout the officers and crew of the World War II fleet submarine:

> The embodiment and personification of this perspective [the spirit of the submarine] is the Captain. His men and his ship reflect his will, and a properly organized crew operates with the unity of purpose of an ant colony. Whatever the state of the individual and of internal affairs, the composite exterior is smooth, unruffled; it acts under a single directive force – a single brain – the Captain's.[43]

This observation also explains why attitudes toward the individual enemy combatants varied so greatly among submarines. Captain Robert D. Risser, Captain of the USS *Flying Fish*, wanted to rescue Japanese sailors from a transport his submarine had sunk. He spent hours calling out to the enemy in the water in fragments of Japanese he had learned from a book. He asked them to come to the sub, encouraged them not to be afraid, and promised that they would not be harmed. Only one accepted his offer, and while onboard the Captain treated and ordered the prisoner be treated with dignity and humanity.[44]

On the other hand, Captain "Mush" Morton of the USS *Wahoo* had a different attitude toward the shipwrecked enemy. The *Wahoo* had just sunk a Japanese troop transport, and the ocean around the site was covered with soldiers and sailors, many in life rafts and other small boats carried by the transport. Once on the surface, he directed the men topside to machine-gun the boats and the Japanese sailors and soldiers floating in the water. Estimated by Morton at about 9,500 "of the sons-of-a-bitches," this carnage continued until, as Morton said in his patrol report, "After about an hour of this, we destroyed all the boats and most of the troops."[45] George Grider, a junior officer under Morton's command wrote about this incident that these were "nightmarish minutes" and that this incident was evidence of the Captain's "...overwhelming biological hatred of the enemy we were only now beginning to sense..."[46]

Edward Beach, a noted submarine author, wrote about Commander Dick O'Kane, Morton's executive officer and later Captain of the USS *Tang*. "In passing, it is a curious commentary on O'Kane to note that not once in any of his patrol reports did he capitalize the word "Jap" or "Nip." To him they were "japs," "nips," and "other debris," if he bothered to mention them at all."[47]

The cooperation and complicity of the crew, in both of these examples of apparently humane and inhumane actions, were evidence of the overlay of the Captain's will, attitude, and personality upon the officers and men of his command.[48] Every Captain on any type of ship creates the "personality" of the ship. On the submarine, this effect was exaggerated due to the small size and close interaction of the crew and the dependence on the Captain to safely and successfully complete their mission and return to port in their fragile craft.

Submarine Battle Tactics

Unlike the surface ships that most often moved in a group, sought out the enemy, and engaged them in an extended battle, the fleet submarine at war was like a sniper, a stealthy and solitary hunter. Like the sniper, the sub gathered intelligence on the intended prey, and a patrol location was chosen. The sub then took its position, and once the victim was selected the submarine became invisible and waited, all stealth and no bravado. The 1943 *Bluejackets' Manual* stated that, "Success of submarine operations depends upon stealth, and to avoid having to surface and reveal its presence in order to scan the vicinity, a submarine is equipped with an optical periscope which can be raised above the surface while the submarine is still submerged."[49] When the target was in optimal range, the underwater sniper would strike and move quickly away from the point of attack. This tactical invisibility certainly allowed enemy vessels to be destroyed, but it also caused the opponent to expend valuable military resources to guard against this unseen foe.

The American submarines of the World War II era were able to travel and fight with the fleet but were in almost all cases vastly overmatched in firepower by their intended targets or the targets' escorts. Only their advantage of stealth gave them the upper hand. The attacking submarine's preferred environment was underwater and invisible or, in some cases, surfaced and invisible, but the retreat was always to the safety of the concealing depths. Like the sniper, the submarine lost its advantage at the instant of attack. Its objective was then to regain its stealth, restore its advantage, and, of course, survive. The formula for a successful undersea sniper attack was planning, positioning, waiting, striking, retreating, and re-positioning.[50]

To determine whether or not a submarine's war patrol had been successful or not required some sort of a measure or scorecard, and in World War II that scorecard was tonnage. Tonnage was the measurement of the displacement, in tons, of the enemy vessels that were sunk or damaged and provided a good equivalency to the military value of the vessel. Thus, a Japanese freighter of 5,000 tons was more valuable, and added more to the scorecard than a military patrol craft of 500 tons; though in each case the submarine sank one ship. The displacement or tonnage also provided a guideline to determine whether or not a target was worth expending one or more of their expensive, and in the early days of the war, scarce, torpedoes.[51]

American submarines in the Pacific were primarily commerce raiders. Their mission was to interdict the transportation of goods useful to the Imperial Japanese war effort, such as petroleum, ammunition, and food. Freighters, tankers, and other large cargo carriers were their main targets. As a secondary mission, submarines were ordered to destroy as many smaller, coastal craft as possible. These smaller vessels, some even under sail, considered as a group were a significant conduit for transporting raw materials like rubber, chemicals, and food to the Japanese home islands. Individually not worth the price of a torpedo, these boats were often dispatched with the submarine's main deck gun, anti-aircraft cannons, or other small arms fire, while the submarine was on the surface. Most often, the enemy crew was invited to disembark before the destruction of their vessel was accomplished.

Enemy warships were, for the most part, something to be avoided by the submarine. Exceptions, of course, included irresistible military targets of high value, like an aircraft carrier or a troop transport that, if sunk or damaged, would do measurable damage to the Japanese fighting ability. These tempting prizes were also of much larger tonnage, like the 27,000-ton Japanese aircraft carrier *Shokaku*, sunk by the USS *Cavalla* (SS 244) during what was called the "Marianas Turkey Shoot" on June 19, 1944.[52] Some Captains though, had success against destroyers, the nemesis of the submarine, and even developed a preference for engagements with these fast and deadly ships. The sub USS *Harder* (SS 257), commanded by Captain Sam Dealey, gained the nickname, "The Destroyer Killer" from its penchant for successfully engaging and sinking these dangerous Japanese warships. As was also common, these "dragon slayers," like the courageous Dealey, won glory and were awarded medals, but often did not return. The *Harder*, her crew, and her Medal of Honor-winning Captain remain on eternal patrol.[53]

War Patrols

Submarine missions were divided into discrete periods of time called war patrols. Unlike surface ships with their vast capacity for food, fuel, and weapons storage, the boats had a limited amount of space onboard for the supplies for the men, for the machines, and for the mayhem they hoped to cause. Patrols by necessity had to be restricted to an average of forty-five to sixty days.[54] At the end of that time, the crew would be exhausted and, though still adequately nourished, would be yearning for fresh vegetables and fruits. Commander Edward L. Beach, submarine veteran and author of the novel made into a movie, *Run Silent, Run Deep*, wrote that after returning from a long war patrol, "...it was not uncommon a see a bearded [submarine] sailor, pockets stuffed with apples and oranges, reading letter after letter in quick succession, and munching on a celery stalk at the same time."[55] A short war patrol was around thirty-five days, while some long patrols approached three months. For example, the USS *Flying Fish's* eleventh war patrol was eighty-three days and was considered quite a challenge to the boat and the crew.[56] In February of 1943, *LIFE* magazine published some rare submarine periscope photos of a successful sinking and a romanticized but basically accurate description of a war patrol:

Submarine duty is called the "silent service." Its ships live in secrecy, work in secrecy, die in secrecy. The public cannot know what they are doing. From their island bases they disappear into the Pacific for as long as three or four months. When at last they do come home, their men are pale and tired. But invariably on the ship's conning towers are proudly painted the outlines of five or ten Jap ships, the number corresponding to the number of the subs' sure sinkings.[57]

Periscope photograph of Japanese ship by USS *Snook*
(SS 279), c. September, 1943.
Courtesy SFM

CHAPTER 3

INTRODUCTION TO THE MEN: WARTIME BIOGRAPHIES OF SIX SUBMARINE SAILORS

But we in it shall be remembered;
We few, we happy few, we band of brothers;
for whoever has shed his blood
with me shall be my brother.

William Shakespeare,
Henry V, Act IV

SIX MEN WILL help bring to life the experience of the enlisted sub-mariner in World War II. Through their interviews and their collected letters, the life and experiences of the World War II-era enlisted sub-mariner will be revealed, explained, and understood, with experiences and observations as unique as the men themselves.

Robert Burr, from the state of Oregon, joined up in 1933 and was an eight year navy veteran when America entered the war. He was a Cook on three different S-class submarines before moving into the fleet boats. Burr served on two of these fleet boats during the war and made four war patrols.

George Jones, a farm boy from Arkansas, was an Engineman who made seven war patrols. Three of them were on the World War I vintage S-boats; one on the USS *S-45* (SS 156), and two on the USS *S-38* (SS 143). Jones also served on four war patrols on the USS *Pogy* (SS 266), a brand new fleet submarine.

Ernie Plantz, from Charleston, West Virginia, made two war patrols onboard the USS *Perch* (SS 176) as an Electrician's Mate before his boat was severely damaged in enemy action. The boat was scuttled, and his entire crew was taken prisoner aboard one of the attacking Japanese destroyers. Plantz spent three and a half years as a prisoner of war on the island of Celebes, and he and the crew were only repatriated after the war had ended.

Jeweldeen "Deen" Brown of Missouri was a Radioman and made nine war patrols, eight of them on the famous "gold sub," the USS *Trout*, (SS 202). Arriving in Pearl Harbor on December 11, 1941 to report for duty on the USS *Nevada* (BB 36), a victim of the Japanese attack only days earlier, Brown talked his way into the submarine force by taking advantage of the confusion of the times and the critical need for skilled radiomen.

Warren Wildes from Noank, Connecticut, served as an Electrician's Mate Third Class on the final war patrol of the USS *Flying Fish*, (SS 229). Warren was only eighteen when he reported on board. He only made a single war patrol, but he participated in one of the most dangerous submarine missions of the war as part of a nine boat wolf pack into the Sea of Japan in 1945.

Finally, there was Harry Julian, a high school junior from Deep River, Connecticut, who left his high school class and high school sweetheart to join the navy. He served as a Torpedoman on the USS *Snook* (SS 279) and served onboard for three war patrols. Harry and the *Snook* never returned from their final patrol. What we know of him we know from the collection of his letters he sent home, starting from his first note while on the train to boot camp, to the last goodbye as he departed on eternal patrol.

One thing united these men of disparate locations, backgrounds, and experiences: they all had an ardent desire to serve on submarines. They knew the dangers and the privations they would have to face, and yet they used their skills, their determination, and occasionally their cunning to get on the boats.

CHAPTER 4

"THE JACK-O'-THE-DUST"

Robert Burr in Chief Petty Officer uniform, c. 1944.
Courtesy Robert W. Burr

Name:	*Robert W. Burr*
Born:	*1914*
Joined Navy:	*1933*
Rating:	*Cook / Commissary Steward*
Served On World War II	*USS Rasher (SS 269)*
Submarines:	*Two War Patrols*
	USS Redfin (SS 272)
	Two War Patrols
Service of Note:	*Served on three S-boats*
Left Service:	*Retired, 1956*

ROBERT BURR WAS the "Jack-O'-The-Dust." This expression, first used in the British navy, described a cook's assistant, who would become covered with flour dust while breaking out provisions for the Cook, defined in the Navy's *Bluejackets' Manual* as, "...an appointee of the supply officer and assists in issuing stores and cleaning storerooms."[1] Burr did not join the navy to be a Cook, but in 1933, in the depths of the Great Depression, any job in the navy was a job worth having. In fact, he was on a waiting list for three years before his induction into naval service, but the wait was worth it for Burr, who was disinclined to join his father in the family business. He recalled, "I went in the service because I was born in eastern Oregon. Farmland, I didn't take to [it], my father had a butcher shop, I didn't take to that. So I kind of had an idea it would be good to do something different. That was the navy."[2]

Burr's first duty station was a surface ship, the destroyer USS *Roper* (DD 147). He was the youngest person onboard by a full six years, since during this period between the world wars, enlistments, transfers, and especially promotions had stagnated. On a ship like the *Roper*, men would remain in their original occupation for years; their rank, pay, and possibilities were frozen. While it was not a professionally enriching situation, it enriched their wallets and was certainly preferable to unemployment. Burr remembered, "This is after the war, and nobody ever got rated, and they just hung on, and some guys didn't care anymore about taking the exam, just got in the habit."[3] But Burr was able and eager and was promoted with exceptional speed. He found himself higher in rank than the six- and eight-year veterans onboard the *Roper*; and this was an uncomfortable situation. He wanted to strike, or apply, for a naval occupation, and like any business, there were good jobs or ratings and not so good ones. Burr recollected that in the peacetime environment, all opportunities were limited. "Well, there was nothing I could strike for. Everybody on the ship, like the seaman seconds, they'd been waiting for years, for torpedo gang, or engineers forward or wherever they wanted to go." So Burr became a Cook, but not willingly. He was frank with the officer who recommended him for the position. "I told him, 'I do not want to be a Cook.' He said, 'Well, I can't offer you anything else on the ship.' I said, 'Well, I'll give it a go.' "[4]

His transformation into a Cook began when the Commissary Steward got in a jam and asked Burr if he would help out by being their "Jack-o'-the-Dust." The duties of this peculiar sounding position included getting up early in the morning, before the Cooks reported. If the ship was in port, Robert picked up the milk and the bread needed by the ship that day, brought it back, and stored it. He would also break the stores out for the galley, using that day's menu as a guide for what supplies the Cooks would need to prepare their meals.

Burr, though not in an occupation he would have chosen, was a hard worker, and this trait was noticed by the Executive Officer on the *Roper*, a former submarine sailor now in the surface fleet due to a physical disqualification. This association would be the force that moved Burr into the submarine service. He remembered well the conversation with the Exec:

> And he come [*sic*] up and he said to me, 'You know, you're doing a good job.' I said, 'Well, the only reason I'm doing a good job is because I'm here, and I might as well do it as not do it.' He said, 'I understand.' I asked him right out, 'You've been on submarines?' He said, 'Yes.' I said, 'I wouldn't mind having a shot at that.' He said, 'You mean that?'...So I asked him about that, and he said, 'Okay, you want to go?' And I said, 'Sure.' I believe it was two weeks later I had orders to go to the sub base at Pearl Harbor. [5]

Since Burr was now officially in the Cooks rating, he did not have to go to Submarine School prior to reporting to his first boat. This was not a uniform practice, but it was typical for those in the Commissary, Cook, or Steward ratings to go directly to their submarine assignments without the benefit of the preparatory training. A number of factors were responsible for this practice. First, Cooks could assume their full duties almost immediately upon reporting with very little orientation. Second, the Cook's area of employment was mostly confined to the galley and did not usually involve the remainder of the ship. Thus, they could master all aspects of their workspace fairly quickly due to the fact that their tools of the trade would be similar whether on a surface, shore, or submarine facility. Last, and the least complementary to the naval service, was that these service ratings were comprised of a large percentage of ethnic minorities. In fact, during this time period, African American sailors, for example, were excluded from many other ratings and were often limited to work in these service ratings. As such, they were, in some cases, in the crew but not of the crew, and their exclusion from attending

Submarine School was an example of this. Where the prejudice of the Captain was most intense, African American submariners were denied the opportunity to qualify on submarines or would receive a partial qualification, and their knowledge and skills were restricted to the general areas of their work. In some extreme but fortunately rare cases, black sailors were systematically transferred off of submarine duty.[6]

In 1938, Burr began his first submarine duty as the only Cook onboard the USS *S-24* (SS 129), an S-class boat, the immediate technological predecessor of the American fleet submarine. This boat had been built by the Fore River Shipbuilding Company in Quincy, Massachusetts, and it was commissioned in 1923. Burr joined the forty other men of the crew and learned the ways of this tiny sub as it made its port change from Pearl Harbor, Territory of Hawaii, to New London, Connecticut. As with almost any new sailor learning the ropes, one of them tripped him up. Burr related the story of how he inadvertently found himself experiencing non-judicial punishment, or Captain's mast, and how the Captain firmly but humorously resolved the case:

> Well, they sent me over to get my friend, a seaman named Evans, and bring him back to ship because he hadn't come back. So I got over there, and I got lost, and he came back. The skipper held mast on me, and he said to me, he said, 'Question.' I said, 'Yes, sir.' He said, 'Do you like my boat?' I said, 'Yes sir.' He said — do you know what his answer was? 'Then I'll never see you up here again, will I?'[7]

Burr left the *S-24* on its return to New London in January of 1939 and began his next submarine assignment. After he first transferred to Pearl Harbor and then spent some time in the hospital, he reported onboard the USS *Skipjack* (SS 184), a Salmon class boat, destined to head for the Pacific as part of the Asiatic Fleet. However, Burr was married by this time and did not relish the idea of being separated from his new bride. After serving on the *Skipjack* for a short time, mostly participating in exercises and local operation around the area of the Hawaiian Islands, Burr left the navy. In June of 1939, he returned to Connecticut with his wife, a native of Norwich, Connecticut. Burr had a hard time finding work and finally received some sage advice from the foreman at the Pratt & Whitney[8] plant, where he had gone to apply for a job. He explained, "They said, 'You're a submarine man,' and I was supposed to reenlist. They said, 'Go back to submarines.' Well, I did it. I shipped over in New Haven."[9]

It seemed like good advice, because Burr was sent to Key West, Florida, in January of 1940 to act as a Cook for the British Bahamas Astronomical Expedition as they surveyed ports, harbors, and lighthouses in the Caribbean to ensure their accuracy. This joint American-British project was a pleasant idyll, but Burr wanted to get back to subs and requested a transfer. As often happens in a military bureaucracy — and to borrow an expression from the science fiction writer Robert Heinlein — Burr's records seemed to go from the fairy godmother department to the practical joke department.[10] He was sent to the USS *Hulbert* (DD 342), a former destroyer being converted to seaplane tender (AVP 6) in the New York Navy Yard, and he was placed in a department with men equally unhappy about their situation. Burr recalled, "So they had a Cook on board, the guy didn't cook. You know who helped him? It was me. All the time. I was pretty bitter about things. I imagine my marks got marked down, 'cause I wasn't very happy with it."[11]

Fate again intervened when a buddy suggested that they visit a submarine tender recently arrived in port. As they walked into the tender's commissary office, the sub sailor on duty offered them cigarettes and brought them some coffee. Burr, reveling in the amity of his one-time comrades, said, "Boy, I'm home."[12] He put in for a transfer and was sent to the USS *S-16* (SS 121) and again found himself under the command of A. H. Taylor, his old skipper from the *S-24*. The *S-16* was one of these older model S-boats, launched in 1919, and it was assigned a coastal defense duty during that inter-war period. As one of a small squadron of submarines stationed at the port of Coco Solo, Panama, the *S-16* and her sister boats were responsible for defense of the Panama Canal. Located on the Atlantic side of the canal, the *S-16* would leave the Atlantic side of the canal on patrol on Monday, pass though the canal to the Pacific side, and reverse the trip to be back at Coco Solo on Friday. Burr remembered that during one patrol he neglected a small but important duty as Cook.

And we'd go through the canal like Monday and come back Friday. And Monday and Friday, and that's it. Well, one of the weeks we was out, damned if I didn't forget to get sugar. We had powdered sugar. You ought to have heard the bitchin'.[13]

Even this mistake highlights the lack of storage space and space in general on the older boats. Later fleet-type boats would have, if not ample, at least adequate storage spaces for the supplies needed for the war patrols that extended sometimes over sixty days. Burr, whose submarine experiences include three S-boats and several fleet boats, clearly understood just how limited in space and equipment the older model was:

> Well, you didn't have no place to put anything. On them old boats, all we had at that time was a commercial refrigerator. We barely could carry; when the *24* boat went back to the States, we barely could have enough fresh stuff to get to Panama from San Diego.[14]

The lack of the boat's creature comforts aside, Burr had pleasant, and sometimes idyllic, experiences in this tropical port. Swim calls from the boat and shore and an occasional ride on a sea turtle somewhat made up for the harsher onboard accommodations.

Burr would serve on one more S-boat before the beginning of the war, the USS *S-48* (SS 159), commissioned in 1922, which operated

Burr (on right) with two shipmates enjoying liberty in
Coco Solo, Panama, c. 1939.
Courtesy Robert W. Burr

out of New London, Connecticut, as an anti-submarine training boat. Burr, though thoroughly familiar with these older model submarines, wanted to serve on the newer, more advanced, and, of course, more comfortable fleet boat. "Well, of course the S-boats had no room. They were, like I said, they only carried thirty-five men on the 24 boat," he recounted.[15] He got his chance with an assignment to the USS *Rasher* (SS 269), a *Gato*-class submarine. The *Gato* class was the first class to fully incorporate all of the definitive characteristics of a fleet submarine. Their speed, range, and armament made them able to support operations with the capital surface ships or to operate safely and effectively as a single hunter.

Burr reported to the *Rasher* in Manitowoc, Wisconsin, as a member of the pre-commissioning crew.[16] He had about three weeks to familiarize himself with the layout and operation of this new boat before it was turned over to the navy. His mother, initially against Burr joining

Launch of the USS *Rasher* at the Manitowoc Shipyard,
20 December, 1942.
Courtesy SFM

the submarine force, made the long journey from Oregon to attend the commissioning ceremony. He remembered her saying, "I'm coming over there. I want to see that ship." He continued, "So she did. And she had to ride a troop train, and she said how nice the guys were. They got up and give her a seat. And they took care of her." After the ceremony, Mrs. Burr was asked if she wanted a tour inside the ship. "You don't think I came all the way out here without getting down [on the ship]?" she said. She was helped down the ladder and toured the entire submarine, from the forward torpedo room to the after battery compartment, and ended in the Control Room. Upon arriving in the Control Room, Burr's mom looked around and said, "Well, I think this ship needs a prayer." Burr reminisced, "And so she said her prayer. I often wonder if that's why it was a successful ship."[17]

Burr, already a nine-year veteran of the navy, was now ready to trade the relatively safe life of the peacetime submariner for the dangerous life aboard an American fleet submarine on war patrol. The *Rasher* had a front row seat to the action and, depending on which one of the various submarine scorecards was used during the war; the *Rasher* would end up in either first or second place with respect to tonnage and number of ships sunk. Only the USS *Flasher* (SS 249) would rival her, sinking over 100,000 tons of enemy shipping.[18] Burr didn't have to wait long to experience some action. He talked about his and the *Rasher's* first war patrol:

> Well, on the first run we went out, and we started to come back through Lombok straits; that's the strait up north of Australia. Going in the [Java] sea, into Borneo and up Borneo on the other side. When we came back, the Japs had several destroyers, and they were really raising hell. So one of them got on our tail; stayed there for a couple days, kept us down. All that time we stayed down I think. Finally he left, and he left a small ship [behind] that could make about the same speed that we could. And they waited until he got far away, and they surfaced. And I saw it go up in temperature to 144 degrees [F] in the battery compartment. That's hot. And those gases are the big problem when you think about it.[19]

Low on fuel, the *Rasher* tried to reach a friendly port in Australia. At one point, the main engines would no longer run due to insufficient fuel, and the *Rasher* proceeded on her "dinky" engine; a small auxiliary engine capable of only extremely low speed. Radio messages were continually sent to alert Allied planes to the *Rasher's* presence. Throughout the war, American submarines were in constant danger of being attacked by enemy and friendly aircraft. Identification procedures were technologically very crude, and the pilots tended to, as the saying goes, shoot first and ask questions later. Burr and the *Rasher* ran into one such pilot while on the surface near Australia.[20] The hull of the ship had been washed clean of any identifying markings, and their attempts to launch signal flares were unsuccessful. Finally, the crew attempted to seek the shelter of the depths as the plane began its attack run. Burr vividly recalled this terrifying experience:

> And that thing just kept coming. The officer of the deck was up there, and finally he just couldn't take it any longer. And he gave the word for diving. Well, we'd already got the word to dive, but couldn't do it because the hydraulic plant had been secured, and it hadn't picked up yet. And they never really trained us for hand dive, you know? Not that much....But anyhow, he came down off the bridge, and he said the wrong thing. He said, 'Somebody do something.'[21]

Captain Hutchinson heard the officer of the deck's plea and immediately came to the Control Room. "Take it easy, we're going down one way or the other," he sardonically said to his second in command.[22] Burr and the crew were doing all they could to get the boat under water, and the Captain recognized this. In addition to the slowness of the dive due to the out-of-service hydraulic plants, fleet boats naturally tended to "hang" for a moment and pause in their dive once their decks were awash. This has been postulated to have been due to the "increased volume of the conning tower appurtenances"[23] slowing an already slow crash-dive time. This rational explanation was of no comfort to the crew of the *Rasher* as they fought for submerged safety. For wartime submariners, even those who had grown used to enemy depth charging, being caught defenseless on the surface was a terrifying experience. Burr distinctly remembered his own fear and that of the crew:

> So we're all standing there. This went on for some time, you know, we're waiting to get killed, right? If I was ever scared, I

was that scared, but I must have been awful nervous, probably just like everybody else. One guy peed all over himself.[24]

The boat made it to a depth of fifty feet before the pilot dropped his load of three one hundred and fifty pound bombs. They landed alongside and rattled the *Rasher,* but the encounter caused no damage other than a few shattered light bulbs and the end of one officer's submarine career. For the panic that officer of the deck exhibited when he asked "somebody" to do "something," the Captain had him removed from the submarine force upon their return to port.

This war patrol, in addition to being extremely perilous, was also of unusually long duration. Burr agreed, "Yeah, that's a long time. You get along, or you don't get along. Look at somebody after sixty days, like what we were doing during the war wasn't even funny, if you stop and think."[25] Also, with experiences like the run-in with a "friendly" plane and the almost commonplace event of being depth charged, it would seem that World War II submariners would have lived in a constant state of fear. But Burr discussed the almost philosophical attitude that submariners had toward the dangers of submarine life and enemy attack:

I never thought about dying all the time I was on the boat. Ain't that something? Never gave it a thought. And we laughed it off and went about our business, that's all we could do. We had some close ones, you know, like a lot of depth charges and things but nothing that — you've got a depth charge, you didn't know when, but it wasn't going to kill you.[26]

Burr spoke about a phenomenon that was apparently common to most successful submariners. There was literally a single moment, almost an epiphany, when the new submariner integrated all of his fears, concerns, and apprehensions about sailing beneath the waves, and then moved on, never to dwell on it again. Whether it was a psychological accommodation or an assertion of young men's bravado, this phenomenon was universal and necessary. One unusual benefit of the danger of submarine duty was that it did not generate the maimed and disabled veterans the way the land-based or even the surface navy did. Lists of wartime recipients of various navy medals and awards indicate that a disproportionally lower percentage of submarine sailors were awarded the Purple Heart, the medal denoting the recipient received a wound in combat, compared to their surface fleet comrades.[27] It was live or die, return or be declared "overdue and presumed lost." Burr thought this was true, and he shared his feeling with his spouse. "I said to my wife when we went to sea, I said, `If I get back, I'll be in one piece.' "[28]

One of Burr's shipmates didn't come back, and he was literally the only man onboard his ship that died during the war. Tragically, this fatality was during a training exercise and not due to enemy action. Burr sadly recalled the specifics of this unfortunate event while discussing the hazards of being topside during a submarine dive:

> …when they sounded that diving alarm, you had only seconds to get on down below, right now. On the second run, we were off of Australia to make a dummy practice because we had this new skipper here, see? I had a new skipper and new quartermaster; quartermaster used to check them off. Nobody checked off the guys on the bridge, and we left one man aboard, in the water. We picked him up two hours and fifteen minutes later, but he died from exposure; it was very cold. That's the only man that I knew that died. I went up topside and helped best I could. They managed to get him aboard, but it was too late.[29]

Burr had reported on as the only Cook and was responsible for preparing and serving three meals a day for around sixty men. By necessity, he conscripted two of the mess helpers and began training them to be Cooks. Reticent about discussing any of his specialty meals, Burr admitted that he was evidently renowned for his bread baking. "God, I made the bestest [*sic*] bread. And that's all I had time for. They ate every damn bit of it; imagine that, thirty-six, two pound loaves a day. Skipper came back and said, `You've got to do something. We're getting too fat!' "[30] A kindly baker, Burr would ignore forays from the sailors in the engine room, who would steal a loaf or two and a pound of butter before they made their get-away. "I'd never said nothing," Burr said. "I did never make life miserable for the guys." His bread making, in addition to his regular meals, kept Burr busy during all of his waking hours. Even the Captain took note of the quality of his loaves and wanted more:

And he [the Captain] said to me, 'Can't you put sandwiches out?' I says, 'Captain,' I says, 'I'm baking nights. I'm making six runs of bread at night.' You could only make thirty-six loaves, two pound loaves of bread. That's all I could make. I had two ovens, and I'd make six runs to make thirty-six. That's a whole fifty pounds of flour; they ate every bit of it every day. It was good bread...[31]

After the *Rasher's* first war patrol, the Captain was so impressed with the quality of Burr's cooking that it merited mention in his war patrol report: "The general excellence of food throughout the patrol contributed materially to the health and morale of the crew on their first patrol after an extended period of commissioning and training."[32] But even with this extra help, Burr had to work his feet off, literally, to produce this amount of food on the two war patrols he made on *Rasher*. He said, "...my feet swelled up so bad I had to get off, I couldn't even walk." Burr was sent to the hospital and, in an attempt to retain his cooking skill, the Captain came to visit him to implore him to try and make the third war patrol. "I said, I just couldn't stand up. I couldn't do it." he told the Captain. But the Captain was not through bargaining and upped the ante. Burr remembers he said, "... 'if you come back and make a run, you'll get a Silver Star.' They put a lot of Silver Stars out. Well, I didn't do that, because I couldn't. So I suppose I missed out. I had to live without the Silver Star."[33]

Burr recuperated in the hospital, and the *Rasher* went to sea. He slowly regained the full use of his legs and was ready to return to his boat. While he waited, he was sent to a relief crew in Submarine Division 162 and assisted with the upkeep and minor maintenance of boats returning from war patrols. He enjoyed this time and stated, "I had a good time in the relief crew; we were no fools. When I say [I mean] I wasn't getting depth charged, but I didn't stay in there on purpose."[34] The *Rasher* didn't return for Burr, but fortunately it was due to a homeport change and not due to enemy action.

Burr then joined the crew of the USS *Redfin* (SS 272) in January of 1945. The boat was bound for Mare Island, California, and a major overhaul. Part of this overhaul included adding mine detection equipment in anticipation of missions around the home islands of Japan. The outfitting with the anti-mine equipment included several weeks training around San Diego in a simulated minefield, and after successfully proving that they could avoid these dummy mines, the *Redfin* was ready to take on the real thing. Burr's first war patrol on the *Redfin,* the *Redfin's* sixth, was on the west coast of Japan beginning July, 1945. Though no enemy ships were attacked, it was fraught with tension, nonetheless. Burr said about this patrol, "We'd patrol the coast and fish would set it [the mine detector] off. It took about two weeks, we made two runs in two weeks, it was just about all the crew could take. Constant, constant; nothing happened. But, who knew? Don't know where the mine's hidden."[35]

As the war drew to a close, missions for submarines became limited, and the *Redfin's* seventh war patrol was a repeat of her sixth; another search for mines and minefields in anticipation of a possible Allied invasion of the Japanese home islands. The war ended after the dropping of the atomic bombs on Hiroshima and Nagasaki, during this patrol. Burr recalled about this time.

> After making those two runs looking for minefields, we were west of Japan, because of the mines breaking loose we were laying around waiting there to go through once it was safe. Well, during that time they had orders, one time or a couple of times, to watch for dropping the bomb. We didn't see it. But they did have lookouts up there, yes they did.[36]

During the war, mail was a powerful morale builder for many sailors, but apparently not for Burr. Concerning his correspondence with his wife, he said, "Very seldom she wrote a letter. We didn't write back and forth much to one another. What could you say, you know? You weren't allowed to write anything because it was censored." Burr acknowledged that his was a different attitude towards receiving mail but explained, "… but I wasn't one who wrote letters, so I didn't miss them, like a lot of people really missed the mail. Not that I didn't love my wife, it was just that I didn't have feelings that way, you know?"[37] There was no question about Burr's feelings about his wife as was clear when he volunteered, "The wife and I, we were married in 1939. Both of us. She's a few months older than I am, and I am 92, and she's already 93. Ain't that something? All that time we had a wonderful life together."[38]

41

After the war, Burr remained in the navy and completed twenty-three years service before he retired in 1956. He finished his career in the New London, Connecticut, area with assignments as the Chief Petty Officer in charge of the Submarine Base galley, on the submarine tender USS *Fulton*, (AS 11), and on the staff of the Commander, Submarine Force Atlantic (SUBLANT). Burr enjoyed his naval career, but with his typical good humor made an ironic comment concerning his naval occupation.

"I made the best of being a Cook. I really had a good career, really, as it turned out. But I didn't like it. I ain't cooked an egg since."[39]

Robert Burr

USS *Rasher* with crew topside.
(CPO Burr eighth from left on the main deck), c. June, 1943.
Courtesy SFM

CHAPTER 5

"THE ARKANSAS PLOWBOY"

George O. Jones, c. 1942.
Courtesy George O. Jones

Name:	George O. Jones
Born:	1919
Joined Navy:	February, 1937
Rating:	Engineman
Served On World War II	USS S-45 (SS 156)
Submarines:	One War Patrol
	USS S-38 (SS 143)
	Two War Patrols
	USS Pogy (SS 266)
	Four War Patrols
Left Service:	Retired, 1956

GEORGE JONES WAS the Arkansas plowboy whose family had emigrated from Mississippi in 1920 when he was still an infant. The boll weevils had ruined that year's cotton crop and the stories of rich land to the west were attractive, so the Jones family literally packed up wagons and moved their entire family and fortunes to a farming community near Clarendon, Arkansas. In the beginning, the land fulfilled its promise, and life was good but certainly not without hardships. When George was three, his mother died, and his father's health deteriorated due to a heart ailment. As the 1920s ended, the effects of the Great Depression were felt on the farm, and a severe drought destroyed the cotton crop in 1930. The Jones family turned to other means to augment their meager farm income. Jones's father, a shrewd trader, had wisely kept his small herd of milk cows and exchanged one of them for a 1930 Model A, one-ton truck. George and one of his brothers instantly became truckers. "My brother and I, we never heard of a driver's license; if you could reach the pedal you could go, you know? So my brother and I were hauling anything that wasn't nailed down that we could make a buck with. And my father was doing the business part, arranging the deals."[1]

As the father's health continued to deteriorate, the Jones family needed to further adapt, so they moved in with George's sister, Pearl, and her husband. By this time, two of the older brothers, Henry Ethel (H.E.) and Robert (R.B.), had married and moved away. Bonnie, the remaining older brother, soon joined the Civilian Conservation Corps (CCC) in 1936. A portion of his pay was sent directly home and was a great help to the family. George slept on the floor in his sister's house, worked with his brother-in-law, and frequently went back to manage his father's farm. When time and chores permitted, he attended school. One day he couldn't find a decent shirt to wear to school, and that's when Jones realized he needed a plan to improve his current and future possibilities. That plan would feature the United States Navy.

Two days before his seventeenth birthday, Jones was in line at the recruiting office in Clarendon. The line was long since the high level of unemployment created by the Great Depression caused the navy to be an attractive source of employment. The navy also provided a special incentive the other services did not offer. Jones explained, "The Army, you could go in at twenty-one dollars a month, stay thirty years, and still be getting twenty-one dollars a month, you know, at that time. But the navy, you went in at twenty-one dollars a month, and at the end of four months you automatically went to seaman second at thirty-six dollars a month. And I needed the money, because I needed to send my father some."[2]

Jones signed up but was on a waiting list of over one hundred and fifty men. To complete his application, though, the recruiter needed his father's signature, as Jones was under the age of 18. Since his father was virtually bedridden by this point, the recruiters agreed to travel to the sister's farm to complete the paperwork. Two Chief Petty Officers arrived during Christmas week of 1936 with the incomplete forms, an empty pickup truck, and big appetites. A while later they left with the forms completed, a good portion of a generous country dinner in their bellies, a truck full of surplus firewood, and a bag of turnips, a favorite of one of the Chiefs. Jones remembered, "So they went back, and I guess they liked this old country boy, you know. So I got a letter from them saying that they had a hundred and fifty on the waiting list, and they got a call from the navy for seventeen. They said, "But if you come over on a standby, if somebody fails to show, we can work you in, maybe.' So February 16 was the date, so I'm over there."[3] Jones arrived and was one of three men waiting on standby. Three of the group did not arrive for the roll call, so Jones and the two others completed the group. Sworn in and placed on the train to the U.S. Navy Recruiting Station, San Diego, Jones began his naval career with the sentiment, in his own words, "I joined the navy for God, country, and something to eat."[4]

After his boot camp training was complete, Jones was sent to his first ship, the USS *Bridge* (AF 1), a refrigeration supply ship that had been commissioned in 1916 and had seen service in World War I.[5] At the time he joined the ship, the *Bridge* served the supply needs of the various naval fleet components stationed on the California coast. As the conflict between China and Japan intensified, the *Bridge* was called to join the Asiatic Fleet as an armed supply vessel. Prior to this temporary assignment, the supply needs of the fleet stationed in Chinese waters were served by civilian steamships of the Dollar Line. As these commercial vessels came under fire, it became necessary to replace them with true combatants.

The *Bridge* docked in Shanghai at the Texaco docks on the Whangpoo River on the night of November 7, 1937. Jones recalled the night sky "lit up with exploding shells" as the Japanese forces battled the Chinese defenders, and the fighting raged around Shanghai. During his time in the China Theater, America was not at war with Japan, so Jones, and other American sailors on liberty interacted cautiously with Japanese forces as they completed their occupation of the city. He was on station during the sinking of the American river gunboat the USS *Panay* (PR 5) on December 12, 1937, by Japanese forces.[6] The *Bridge*, in Amoy provisioning two riverboats at the time, was summoned back to Shanghai to take on western refugees from the International Settlement. Survivors of the *Panay* were taken onboard her sister gunboat the USS *Oahu* (PR 6) for transfer to the flagship of the Asiatic Fleet, the heavy cruiser USS *Augusta* (CA 31). According to Jones, immediately after the sinking of the *Panay,* a Japanese heavy cruiser passed within range of the *Augusta's* guns. The Captain had his crew at battle stations and was ready to order the guns to fire when Admiral Yarnell, commander of the Asiatic Fleet laid his hand on the Captain's shoulder and said, "Don't do it, Captain." When the Captain replied, "They sank one of ours." Yarnell answered, "Wait for Washington."[7] Diplomacy quelled the anger engendered by this incident, and a relative peace would exist for four more years.

On March 4, 1938, her storerooms near empty, the *Bridge* made preparations to head back home. Jones, although reasonably content as a seaman first class on the deck force, recollected, "I wanted to learn a trade that would help me when I got out. I didn't want to go back to farming..."[8] Driven by his eagerness to gain a skill, coupled with his affinity for the engineering ratings, Jones believed the best way to enter one of these technical ratings would be through volunteering for submarines. He did just that upon his return from the China Station. Jones recalled:

> So I thought if I could get Submarine School and, if I could, get Diesel School. I had heard very little about submarines, but I had been aboard one. When I was going through — no, when I was on the bridge, we were tied up in San Diego when the old "S" boats came back from someplace, Pearl Harbor I think. One of them

came into San Diego and tied up right near our ship. So I went over and went through it. I think I only seen one guy down below. He showed us everything we wanted to know all the way through the boat, you know. And I said, "Jeepers, I don't see no officers." I thought that would be good duty, to me it looked like good duty.[9]

Jones had in mind that he might more easily be accepted into an engineering rating if he got some experience before being transferred. During this time, acceptance into a rating or occupation was by no means assured. A sailor without prior training was expected to apply, or "strike," for a rating, both on the surface and in the submarine fleet. In addition to various means of identifying aptitude, one means of improving chances for being accepted was to have worked within that rating. Jones said:

So I requested from the Engineering Officer on that ship that if it was approved for me to go to Sub School that he'd give me a trial down in the reciprocating steam engine room. And so he agreed. It would be a trial after NAVPERS [Naval Personnel Office] approved the transfer. They said to wait until the ship reached the East Coast before transfer. So I went in the engine room on a trial basis to help them out through the [Panama] Canal. The day they transferred me to Submarine School from Norfolk, they changed my rate over from Seaman First to Fireman Second.[10]

On April 24, 1938, now Fireman Second Class George Jones stepped off the train on State Street in New London, Connecticut, as a new student in Submarine School. The first qualification a prospective submariner had to master was in the Escape Training Tank, a one hundred foot tall landmark on the Submarine Base in Groton, Connecticut. This cylindrical tower of water provided a land-based opportunity to screen out candidates who could not or would not withstand the stress and physical pressure of ascending to the surface from a hypothetical submarine stranded one hundred feet down. First, the students were placed in a chamber and subjected to increased air pressure to simulate the actual pressure at one hundred feet. Once past this exam, candidates would be led up the tower. They would use a rescue breathing device called a Momsen Lung and would descend to the eighteen foot level and

ascend correctly, breathing out all the way up. Jones passed this qualification on April 27, 1938.

Submarine school consisted of classroom and practical training.
In the classroom, students like Jones were taught topics like submarine history, buoyancy, and general boats systems. Four older R-class
boats were assigned to the Submarine School as "school boats."
These boats, built in the years immediately following the Great War,
were working relics of an earlier technological period. Riveted, not
welded, hulls, manually operated valves, no air conditioning, and no
hydraulics were just some of the features that made these boats

R-class school boat traveling up the Thames River with the
Groton Bank in the background c. 1940.
Courtesy SFM

unique in a 1930s modern navy. But they were good enough to serve
as instructional platforms for these new submarine recruits.

Classes of students, supervised by experienced instructors,
would take these school boats out into Long Island Sound and practice maneuvering, diving, and surfacing under controlled conditions.

During one of these sessions, Jones's training for the day was cut short by an emergency message from one of the escort vessels that always accompanied the school boats. "Surface immediately and return to port" was the direction from the escort USS *Semmes* (AG 24), an old World War I four-stack destroyer.[11] The emergency that ended the day's training was the sinking of the USS *Squalus* (SS 192) in Portsmouth, New Hampshire, while on sea trials, with the loss of twenty-six crewmen. With the help of the *Semmes* and the USS *Falcon* (ASR 2), also from New London, the thirty-three men trapped in the intact forward compartments of the *Squalus* were saved, and the incident became part of submarine and naval rescue legend.[12] The students were made aware of the disaster as they marched back to class, and two of Jones's classmates had a drastic reaction:

> We, the students, fell in line to march back to our classroom. Two of my classmates told our instructor that they wanted to go to the personnel office instead. He asked why, they said they wanted to return to their ship, they did not wish to continue Submarine School. We went to the classroom. They went to the personnel office. We didn't see them again. We were kept in the classroom while the personnel office processed their transfer papers, arranged transportation, took them to the barracks to retrieve their belongings, and shipped them out, back to the cruiser they came from. Our instructor told us the personnel office entered in their records, reason for transfer, one word, "squalusites," in red ink.[13]

All of the New London school boats, like herd animals rushing to the side of a fallen mate, were sent to Portsmouth to aid in the rescue efforts. Jones attended his first submarine memorial service to pray for the rescue of those trapped on the *Squalus* and for the repose of the souls of those lost. With the school boats gone, training focused on classroom topics, and the history of submarine disasters was one of interest to both the students and the instructors.

Jones graduated from "Blow and Vent College," as the old timers called the Sub School, on Friday, June 16, 1939. Many of his classmates were sent directly to the fleet for submarine duty availability, and some went to Radio or Battery Schools. Jones began Submarine Diesel School that next Monday, and his assignment to this school, assuming successful completion, assured his membership in the Engineman rating. This task proved more difficult for him than Sub School had been. Focused on keeping the farm and his family financially secure during the worst of the Great Depression, Jones had not given full attention to his classroom studies before joining the navy. This lack of preparation, especially in mathematics and science, became evident to him during the highly technical Diesel School. A week in the hospital battling a persistent leg infection and the ensuing absence from class made a difficult task almost impossible. One failed test away from expulsion, Jones buckled down and achieved a passing score on the final exam. On September 25, 1939, Jones graduated from Submarine Diesel School, eleventh out of twelve, but passed and ready for his first submarine assignment.

Using trains, taxis, and their thumbs, Jones and two other graduates made their way to Norfolk, Virginia, for transport to the Submarine Base at Coco Solo, Panama. Jones's submarine service was nearly stillborn as he and one of his shipmates were temporarily assigned to the submarine rescue and salvage ship, the USS *Mallard* (ASR 4) a converted minesweeper, that carried out target towing and diver training services for ships stationed there.[14] Jones, though itching to get on submarines, remembered his *Mallard* shipmates as "one of the best crews I ever sailed with," and he benefitted from the experience in these associations and in the ability to gain more training in his rating:

> What it was, I'm sure, was they needed me on the *Mallard* so they said they'd send me on there 'til they had a vacancy. Well, I damn near got stuck on there, but I was on there four months. So I managed to talk my way out of that one. But while I was on the *Mallard*, they brought all those divers that had dove on the *Squalus* down, came aboard the *Mallard* for duty. And I got to be friends with them, so I got a lot of firsthand information about the *Squalus*.[15]

On March 19, 1940, about four and a half months after reporting to the *Mallard*, Jones was transferred to the USS *S-45* (SS 156), one of the older S-boats assigned to Submarine Squadron Three at Coco Solo. Commissioned in 1925, the *S-45* was effectively a World War I submarine that would do its best to meet the challenge of a technologically superior opponent. While on the *45* boat, Jones qualified in submarines, passed the examination for Petty Officer Second Class, and participated in several deployments to ports on both sides of the Panama Canal.

When Jones heard about the Japanese attack on Pearl Harbor, the *S-45* was tied up at the pier on Ordinance Island in Bermuda. Plans to return to New London were scrapped, and Jones and the boat proceeded again to Coco Solo. After a rushed mechanical overhaul and loading of stores, the *S-45* transited the canal and took up patrol station on the Pacific side. In the days immediately following the surprise attack, it was uncertain where the next blow would fall. Invasion of the continental United States was not ruled out, and neither was a destructive attack on the Panama Canal, a vital Allied naval transport route. The plucky old submarine established a semicircular patrol pattern about one hundred miles off the Panama coast, ready to do its best to repel any Japanese attacking force.[16]

Once the remainder of December and January 1942 had passed, it became clear that there would be no attack on the canal, and the *S-45* returned to the base at Coco Solo. There, the *S-45* was reconstituted into a new submarine group, Submarine Division 53, consisting of a submarine tender, the USS *Griffin* (AS 13), and six submarines; the USS *S-42, S-43, S-44, S-45, S-46,* and *S-47*. At the beginning of March, this new division transited the canal and made their way through newly hostile waters to arrive for duty at Brisbane, Australia, forty-four days later in mid-April.

The *S-45* began its first war patrol on May 12, 1942 in Japanese-controlled waters around the Solomon Islands and passed through the Coral Sea a mere four days after the famous battle of the same name. Their mission was to seek and engage enemy shipping and to rendezvous at Buka Island on a proscribed date to pick up two Australian coast watchers who had been observing Japanese activity from the cover of the hills and jungles. Due to the frequency and intensity of depth charge attacks on the submerged boats while passing through this area, Buka forms part of the boundary of the passage between New Britain and New Ireland that became known to the submariners as "Ash-Can Alley." Tiny Buka alone was home to a Japanese Naval base that possessed navy fighter planes and short-range anti-submarine bombers equipped with depth charge bombs.

The *S-45* took up station and tried unsuccessfully to make contact with the coast watchers. After waiting passively for two nights, the boat finally surfaced and flashed its signal light at the beach to no avail. The Captain observed the masts of three Japanese destroyers making their way around the island and believed the submarine had been detected. Past their schedule and failing at their mission, the *S-45* attempted to make a rapid departure from this dangerous area. Relative stealth and control became chaos. Jones recalled:

> Evidently, they didn't know we were there, though. So we went to dive, and everything on the boat crapped out. We dove, but the bow planes crapped out, what the hell else? Oh, the clutch on the engine, the body-bound bolts came loose, you know, they sheared off. So after that, we only had one engine.[17]

Alone and in distress, the *45* boat could have used some assistance or support. So thought the Captain when he ordered the Radioman, a Chief Petty Officer, to send a radio message calling for help. The Chief appeared to comply, but soon reported to the Captain that due to moisture in the transmitter, the radio was out of commission. But Jones believed that there was another reason for the radio's condition:

> He blew the transmitter up. I believed him when he told me later in confidence that he did it intentionally, because he said, "With those three destroyers coming over there," he said, "if I'd have opened up that transmitter, they'd have been right on us and here everything was pooped out." Well, I believed him, and I think he did, but he claimed that moisture got in there and blew it up. And inside that pig-iron hull, you did get a lot of moisture.[18]

One engine out of commission, inoperative bow planes, and no radio were the major problems, but certainly not the only ones. A mistake with a valve line-up caused the remaining fresh water to be pumped overboard, the stores refrigerator broke down, and several tainted cans of ham exploded, sending the smell of rotted meat throughout the boat. A line from the war patrol report highlights the general environmental conditions on all S-boats and underscores how this hastened the deterioration of the material and morale. "The habitability of the boat was very poor due to the high humidity. Boat temperature, wet and dry bulb, was taken daily. The average boat temperature was 96° F, with a relative humidity of approximately 96%".[19]

The *S-45* ended their arduous, challenging, and unsuccessful patrol on June 19 after thirty-nine long days, nine days overdue. Due to their lateness and lack of radio communication, the boat had been considered lost by the squadron commanders. Jones and his crewmates emerged from the boat blinded by the Australian sun. They were pale, dirty, greasy, and weak from the odyssey of limping back from patrol with little food or water onboard. A month of relative ease and recreation in a Rest Camp cured most, if not all, of the crew's aliments. The *S-45*, on the other hand, required more than just rest before she could return to sea.

Jones heard that another S-class submarine, the USS *S-38* (SS 143), was in need of a qualified Throttleman, so he made a pre-dawn mission to talk to that boat's Engine Room Chief. After a night on liberty and, in his own words, with a "hint of alcohol" on his breath, he stated his desire to transfer onboard the *38*. The Chief told him to return to his boat and to say nothing. Only a few hours later, back on the *S-45*, Jones was summoned before the Captain. "Do you want to go to that Asiatic Broken Down Boat?" the Captain asked him. "Yes, sir," Jones replied. "Why?" queried the Captain. Jones answered, "Because I want to get off this State Side Broken Down Boat, sir." The Captain stormed off, and the Executive Officer approached Jones and asked him what the Captain had said. When Jones informed him that he hadn't said anything, the Exec said, "Well, I guess that means you are transferred, go pack your things." Sometime after Jones reported onboard the *S-38*, he learned the whole story of his hurried transfer. The Captain of the *S-38*, facing an imminent deployment and short one Throttleman, made an early morning visit to the squadron command to plead his case. Captain Eddy of the *S-45* was awakened to participate in this dawn discussion, with the resultant order that left him short one valuable crew member. Jones believed the abrupt awakening and order to give over a highly qualified man may have been the cause of his terse farewell.[20]

Jones began his second war patrol, and the *S-38's* seventh, on July 28, 1942, as one of the Throttlemen in the engine room of the *S-38.*, He was also somewhat of an engine room supervisor, with an assistant Oiler named "Lug" Lewis. During his watch, the Throttleman was in

USS *S-38* (SS 138) at sea, c 1939.
Courtesy SFM

charge of ensuring that the diesel engines were running properly and making necessary configuration changes when direct propulsion or battery charging was ordered. The Oiler, in addition to lubricating moving parts and assisting the Throttlemen, maintained the equipment and looked for leaks after depth charge attacks. Jones had chosen his new assignment well, as the *S-38* was a tight boat with a very well-organized and qualified crew. He found out just how comprehensive submarine qualifications were on the *S-38* during his first Throttleman watch:

> I was on watch when Chow went down at 5:30 PM, and I knew Verzivielt (called "Verzy") was sleeping, and I didn't want to have him called, but I was hungry, when a large man came through the hatch and said "Go eat Jonesy, I'll relieve you." I knew that there was a First Class Engineman by the name of Fossberg in the Aux-

iliary Gang and figured he was probably a qualified Throttleman, so I turned the Watch over to him and went in the Mess Hall and sit down to eat. I could see through the engine room hatch from where I was sitting. A Fireman by the name of Ashcroft was sitting by me, and I ask him, "Is that Fossberg that relieved me?" And he said "Hell no, that's Barnum, our First Class Radioman." I started coming up out of my seat to run for the engine room, and he put his hand on my shoulder and said, "Sit down and eat, he can dive the engine room if the diving alarm goes." I went back to eating. What a crew![21]

The *S-38's* patrol area for this patrol was again the straits between New Britain and New Ireland in the vicinity of Rabaul, on the island of New Britain, the location of an important Japanese military installation. Late on the night of August 8, Jones and the crew made a sound directed attack on a large vessel escorted by a Japanese destroyer. Two torpedoes were fired, and two explosions were heard and soon drowned out by the cheering of the crew. The boat was able to make its escape undetected and heard only a single depth charge explode in the far distance, coupled with the unmistakable sounds of a dying ship. Much later, they discovered that their tiny submarine had sunk the 5,600-ton Japanese troop transport, *Meiyo Maru*, loaded with troops and armament. This lucky shot may have delayed this invasion force on its way to Guadalcanal. The delay gave the Marines there precious time to strengthen their defenses.[22]

Two nights later, the *S-38* returned to the scene of the sinking to continue searching this previously lucrative hunting ground. A Japanese destroyer, perhaps even the one that was protecting the ship that Jones's boat sank, pounced on them from out of the darkness. Trying to avoid the destroyer's desperate attempt to ram the fragile boat, Jones and the crew dove the boat to thirty-two feet, periscope depth, in a brief thirty-two seconds. Jones, along with the whole engine room crew, had a busy half minute available to secure the engines and the distilling units, disengage the clutches, and close the sea water valves. During this frantic activity the destroyer dropped three depth charges close by, the first Jones had experienced. Ironically, as the agents of death exploded around his ship, Jones smiled broadly as he ran from task to crucial task:

So anyway, when he run over us, he went right where we had been before we submerged, he rolled off three depth charges. That didn't scare me because I was so busy, you know, I didn't get scared, and I was smiling all the way through it according to one of the other guys. They got rid of that smile later.[23]

In the post-action war patrol report, the commanding officer of the *S-38*, Captain Munson, specifically noted Jones's competence, writing, "...the engineering gang doing a particularly smart job of securing a charge, securing the evaporator, securing the air compressor, getting the starboard tail clutch in, and getting the port motor started in manual control, and getting us a 32-second dive...."[24]

Their mission accomplished, the *S-38* began its return voyage home, arriving in Brisbane, Australia, on August 22, 1942. Though the war patrol report mentioned some material problems, Jones considered this war patrol almost a pleasure cruise after experiencing all the breakdowns during the patrol on the *45* boat. On the pier were the submariner's standard welcome home gifts: a band and dignitaries, fresh fruit, lettuce, and, of course, ice cream.

Boat refitted and replenished, crew rested and restored, and orders received, the *S-38* left for its eighth war patrol on September 21, 1942, in company with the USS *S-41*. This mission began in Brisbane and was more of a reconnaissance mission. As such, the *S-38* put to sea with only four torpedoes to "avoid depleting the supply at Brisbane." The patrol ended uneventfully in Pearl Harbor, where the boat proceeded to San Diego for a major overhaul. Their first stop was at the island of Nouméa, in the region of New Caledonia, an Allied port and an opportunity for the *S-38* to refuel and take on extra stores. The variety of naval vessels anchored there impressed the young George Jones. He recalled, "God, I've never seen so many ships; a huge harbor. And for the first time we see our navy, mostly troop ships."[25]

The boat proceeded to their patrol area around Tarawa about six weeks before the Marines made their famous landing and surveyed the harbor and environs. The Captain of the *S-38* spotted a tanker in the harbor accompanied by a destroyer. Later analysis indicated that the enemy vessels probably observed the American submarine, causing the Japanese tanker to make preparations to appear she was getting underway. This target proved too tempting for the Captain of the *S-38*, and he ordered three torpedoes to be fired at the target. The submarine crew was unaware there was a submerged reef between the submarine and its target. When the three torpedoes exploded harmlessly on the reef, Japanese planes from the other side of the island appeared and began their attack run on the now-disclosed boat. The *S-38*, like most S-boats, had an idiosyncrasy that if the boat rapidly fired three torpedoes they could lose depth control and broach, or unexpectedly surface. Jones, due to his previous S-boat experience, was asked to take the Stern Planes for his battle station. His experience and skill contributed significantly to the *S-38's* survival during this encounter with these Japanese aerial anti-submarine forces. As the *S-38* wallowed on the surface, struggling for depth control, the enemy planes dropped twenty-two depth bombs around her. All of Jones's experience on his battle station was required as the force of the explosions pounded the ship:

So I had took the stern planes [during the attack]. The bubble tube busted, and the liquid hit me right in the face. I had a vision when that happened of the pressure hull opening up and a shot of water coming through. And my stomach went in hard knots, and the old man said, "Take it, we're broached." We'd fired three fish and couldn't control the ballast, you know. We broached and those S-boats didn't have a negative tank, so, God they — we had shrapnel holes in the fairwater around the conning tower. They didn't go through the conning tower but around it. They had a main drain run along the keel of the ship that you could pump bilges through and all that; they knocked holes in that. So we wound up in a hell of a mess. They beat the shit out of us.[26]

With bombs falling in the water around them, and light bulbs inside the ship imploding "like if you grabbed them and squeezed them," as Jones said, the *S-38* dove to one hundred feet, then blew back up to seventy-five as the Captain and crew fought this see-saw battle for the safety of the depths because. As Jones remembered, "...we wanted to go deep. We wanted to get away from that surface." He was terrified and distinctly recalled the feeling of being the object of the enemy's wrath. "I felt a hot flush start at the top of my head and run all the way down through my body and come out through the bottom of my feet as my guts cramped into a hard ball.

And a deep feeling came over me that 'Someone up there is trying to kill me.' It wasn't they are trying to kill us, it was 'Me'..."

As the bombs continued to fall, the Captain ordered, "Take her down to one hundred and fifty feet," because he knew that once in the dark safety of the regions below one hundred feet, they could most likely relax a bit and relieve some of the tense battle stations, like the ones Jones manned on the stern planes. Jones recalled, "The Diving Officer, 'Red' Lenox, tried to repeat the order and said, 'Take her down to 32 foot - to hell with the pressure.' He meant 150 feet. This saying became known throughout the Submarine Navy later." Jones used his senses and his experience to operate these planes since his normal guide, the "bubble," had broken during the bombing, and he was, in his words, "having to go by the angle we were, feeling with my fanny..."[27]

Jones unsteadily returned to his engine room and found the Oiler on duty sitting on top of and holding onto the oil purifier. He laughed at Jones's wobbling gait, his balance impaired by a combination of fear and the repeated depth charge explosions. "Did you check for leaks?" Jones asked him. "Ha, ha, ha," giggled the Oiler, his equilibrium also shaken by the explosions, "I can't get up."[28] Jones heard water running and jacked up a deckplate nearest the sound, where he found the packing gland loose on a four-inch compensating water valve. After tightening the gland and stopping the leak, Jones was replacing the deckplate when another depth charge went off and caused the deckplate to drop and gash his shin almost down to the bone.

Since the S-boats did not usually carry even a Pharmacist's Mate in their crew, it was up to Jones, the Executive Officer, and a meagerly supplied medical locker to devise a remedy. In this era before the mass production of antibiotics, the best they could come up with was some Tincture of Merthiolate[29] and a bandage. However, in the Tropics, with no air conditioning and no effective way to maintain cleanliness, the cut swelled, turned white, and became infected. The old hands onboard immediately recognized this as a Tropical Ulcer, a condition that would remain with Jones until he was able to reach land and medical attention.

However, before any remedy could be obtained, the boat had to reach port. When Jones found the main engine clutch damaged, he was uncertain if this would ever happen. The 38 had a friction clutch, and the repeated depth charges had damaged it to the point where it would not effectively engage. The clutch was used to connect the engines to the propeller shaft. So without an operable clutch, the *S-38* could not maintain both the ability to choose to propel the boat or to charge the batteries with the engines. They chose the former and installed shims in the clutch teeth, effectively making a permanent decision to run on the surface driven by the diesel engines. They left their station in the Solomon Islands and traveled on the surface, night and day, through enemy territory. As Jones remembered, "So we run from there all the way to Pearl Harbor on the surface, scared to death."[30]

The *S-38* made it safely to Pearl Harbor for some rest and recreation for the crew at the Royal Hawaiian Hotel and for some desperately needed repairs for the boat. The small S-boat was an unusual sight for the Pearl Harbor sailors, but any humor the sight of this diminutive submarine might have provoked was silenced by the four Japanese flags painted on the conning tower. They represented the four ships the *S-38* had sunk, one since Jones had joined the crew.[31]

When both were sufficiently restored, the boat and crew continued on to San Diego. Once relieved from shipboard duty, Jones sought out some more formal medical attention for his leg, and when that proved ineffective, applied a remedy of his own devising:

> I went up to the hospital, yes. And they'd never heard of a tropical ulcer, and they started picking at it, and God, they really got it messed up. So the next day I went over to the Gold Rail [Bar]. We decided Eddy's Round Bar was too big for us. We'd meet down at the Gold Rail. The crew hung together, whatever bar, you'd find the whole crew — that is, all that was free. I went down and sat at the bar and ordered. We all drank Scotch and Coke; White Horse and Coke. I don't know who the hell come up with that, but everybody thought it was great. So I put my leg up on the stool next to me with that big bandage and I ordered two; one for me, and one for my leg. And when the bartender served me the drinks, I proceeded to drink one and pour the other one on the bandage on my leg. I kept doing this for the next four days, at which time I removed the bandage, and my leg was cured. It cured it, it worked.[32]

After an extensive overhaul in San Diego, the *S-38* returned to Pearl Harbor, where Jones was transferred to a Relief Crew 43, just prior to the boat's departure on its ninth war patrol on June 25, 1943. While in the relief crew, Jones performed engine overhauls and other related work on boats back from patrol. After about two months of this duty, his squadron received a request from the new fleet submarine USS *Pogy* (SS 266), just returning from her second war patrol, for replacement personnel.

Jones was a little apprehensive about being asked to transfer. While the S-boats he served on had two inline eight cylinder NELSCO diesel engines, the fleet boats had four V-sixteen General Motors diesel electric engines; Jones was not familiar with these newer model engines. The differences did not stop there. As a Throttleman on an S-boat, Jones was responsible for operating the clutch and controls to actually power the sub. On a fleet boat, the four big engines just made electricity, which was then directed to either the propulsion motors or the storage batteries. The Throttleman position still oversaw engine room operations, but the motor controls, located in the Maneuvering Room, were operated by Electricians.

The *Pogy* left Pearl Harbor on September 9 for her third war patrol with Jones aboard. Jones spent this patrol learning the new engines and getting to know his new crew. Since there were at least twenty more people onboard the fleet boat, this took a little longer than it would have on the *S-38*. During this patrol, the *Pogy* sank one ship, the 7,000-ton freighter *Maebashi Maru*.[33] Though the sub was not severely depth charged during this patrol, Jones learned that the fleet boats "took a punch" a bit differently than did the older subs. When the *Pogy* shot at a ship and missed, the intended target returned the favor with three depth charges. Jones remembered:

> This was my first experience in battle on a fleet boat, but my memories was [sic] of the terrible beating I had taken on the *S-38* boat at Tarawa, and I kept waiting for the deck plates to move out from under my feet. I found out the fleet boats being much larger than the S-boats, they had much more resistance to moving sideways in the water. So instead they would suddenly squat when getting depth charged, if the explosion was close.[34]

Sinking the single Japanese ship was enough for the patrol to be declared successful, and after a routine rest period, the *Pogy* was sent back on patrol on November 25, 1943. This run was to be much more productive and much more eventful than the previous one.

On December 7, 1943, the *Pogy* sighted two ships, a large freighter and a submarine tender, underway and escorted by a destroyer. The *Pogy* attacked and immediately sank the submarine tender and damaged the freighter. The destroyer dropped twenty-two depth charges, but none of them were very close to the boat. The Captain found a marginal thermal layer that he jokingly characterized in his war patrol report, "Found 1° negative gradient at 330 feet, so ran at 350, feeling like an elephant under a cabbage leaf." At the end of the attack, the Japanese submarine tender *Soyo Maru* and passenger-cargo vessel *Fukkai Maru* were on the bottom. The commanding officer of the *Pogy's* submarine division humorously noted in his endorsement of the war patrol report, "The first series of attacks took place on 7-8 December and the result was the DD (destroyer) escorting two fine ships had nothing left to escort."[35]

The next encounter for Jones and the *Pogy* occurred five days later, when she took on a troop ship of the *Panama Maru* class in the waters near Palau. The *Pogy's* crew fired three torpedoes at the target, heard two strike the ship, and watched the transport "sag in the middle."[36] Her attack alerted the transport's escort and several harbor patrol vessels. While trying to gain a firing position on a second freighter, the *Pogy* attempted to avoid the sonar ranging patrol craft. The escort vessel dropped twenty-seven depth charges, while the patrol craft, when they thought they had picked up the submarine, would drop groups of two. The transport had been attacked in the early morning, but it was not until the evening, after a long day of cat-and-mouse with the patrol craft, that one of the Japanese boats finally got lucky. Lt. Wright, the Engineering Officer and the officer in charge and Gleason, a crew member and the sound man operating the sonar equipment, were on duty during this close call that Jones described:

So anyway he [Gleason] said, "Mr. Wright, they're pinging on us." Wright said, "Ah, I don't think so." He didn't take no evasive action. And Gleason said, "He's picked us up, he's securing his sound gear and starting to make his run." Wright said, "I don't think so." Gleason threw his headphones down and screamed down the hatch, "Captain to the Conning Tower." And boy that was — saved our lives. The Captain came, boy he hit those stairways really running. He run up and he raised the scope up like that. "Take her down, take her down, take her to three hundred feet!"[37]

The sound man's assertiveness and the Captain's quick assessment saved the *Pogy*, but not until after the patrol craft inflicted some severe punishment. Jones recollected, "They just got it flooded, and he laid three right down us, and so it damaged our torpedo tubes where we couldn't fire torpedoes after that. But he lost us. He was going so fast he couldn't stop."

The Captain planned to wait until dusk and then surface and make a break for the open sea. With anticipated bright moonlight, dusk would be the darkest part of the night. The Captain passed the word to the engine room to have all main engines ready when they hit the surface. Jones had been repairing an engine cylinder damaged in the attack, and had just finished completed reinstalling the head before the call came for full power. He remembered, "And the head cover, we didn't have the final lid on it yet, it threw oil and shit all over the engine room, but we had it running. When we hit the surface there's four main engines [ready]; we lit it off without that lid being on it, the rocker arms was not covered. Threw oil and shit all over, but we got out of there, that was the main thing. We could scrub that oil off the overhead." The patrol boat's attack had also damaged the torpedo tubes. Anticipating another chance at the remaining freighter, the depth spindles[38] had not been withdrawn from any tubes, and the concussion of the depth charges damaged them. Additionally, ballast tank 4A had been ruptured and could not be repaired. The *Pogy* was safe, but due to the inoperable torpedo tubes and leaking tank, she could no longer effectively mount an attack, so the war patrol was cut short.[39]

After a refit period on Midway Island, the *Pogy* left for its fifth war patrol bound for a patrol area around the island of Formosa, now called Taiwan. Arriving on station in mid-January, 1944, the *Pogy* also cruised around the island group of Okinawa Jima, about halfway between Formosa and the home islands of Japan. While off the southern tip of Formosa, the *Pogy* picked up a convoy of nine ships, including two escort vessels. Early in the morning of February 10, the *Pogy* was in position and began her attack on the convoy with a spread of five torpedoes. The first torpedo hit the Japanese destroyer *Minekaze* in her magazine, causing a enormous explosion that obliterated the bow of the warship. As Jones recalled, "The lead fish hit him and blew him sky high. Everything he had must have exploded. Fire and shit went a thousand feet up."[40] The remaining torpedoes hit and sank the 5,500-ton passenger cargo ship *Malta Maru* and damaged another freighter as well.[41]

The engine room gang, including Jones, experienced a different kind of battle than the crew in the Control Room may have. Jones's job was to keep the engines available, to answer all orders, and to be ready to secure them if the order to dive the boat was given. Though one of the crew in the engine room was always on the internal phone system, much of what they knew about the battle as it took place had to be inferred. Jones remembered what it was like in the engine room of a fleet boat during surface-torpedo attack:

> Back in the engine room, we could only guess what was going on. However, we had the phones manned at all times when at battle stations. We would pick up some information from them, plus when word was passed on the 1MC (Loud Speaker), we would either make it out over the noise of the engines or would get the word over the phone.

When the Captain fired the torpedoes, there was a shudder of the boat for each of the torpedoes as they were fired, so we knew how many were fired, and then came the big explosions which shook us, and both the phones and the loud speaker was heard with all types of comments on what was going on. We knew we had fired a total of five torpedoes, we heard that we had fired at two (2) ships and hit three (3) and that the flame from the hit on the destroyer went 1,000 feet high. After the last fish was fired, "Full speed ahead" was rung up on the maneuvering room enunciators, and word came over the speakers, "Maneuvering room, we want to go places." And explosions started going off alongside the boat and the deck plates would jump up and down under our feet. We knew someone was shooting at us, and they were close. I stood between the over speed trips (one for each engine), where I could hold them in to keep them from tripping out if they exceeded the maximum RPM.[42]

During this very successful patrol, the *Pogy* would go on to sink another three freighters; the impressive tally was four ships sunk for

22,311 tons and four ships damaged of 20,184 tons.[43] After a brief stop at Midway to replenish food and fuel, the *Pogy* continued on to end this patrol on March 8, 1944. On this return, the band and dignitaries on the pier were treated to the sight of a broom lashed to the number one periscope, raised high, indicating that the *Pogy* had "swept the oceans clean" of enemy shipping.

Jones departed on his seventh and last war patrol on the *Pogy's* sixth on April 7, 1944. On this patrol the boat sank two freighters, two sizable sampans, and a large Japanese submarine later determined to be the *I-183*, which was believed to be carrying a load of aviation gasoline.[44] On May 16, the *Pogy* used gunfire to stop and sink a twenty-ton diesel-powered sampan. It was fairly routine toward the end of the war for submarines to interdict these paramilitary craft to destroy their potentially important cargo and end their role as provisional patrol and communication ships. What was not routine about this action was the five prisoners taken from the waters around the sampan's floating wreckage. Even more unusual, these sailors did not seem all that eager to escape capture, and Jones explained why:

> Well, it is because, it turned out, these were just fishermen. They didn't give a shit less as long as they could live. Get back to the States. They were scared to death when we brought them aboard. When we were bringing them aboard one of them hollered out, "San Diego." So from then on, his name was San Diego.[45]

The Pharmacist's Mate bandaged up the prisoners' minor wounds and tried to determine if any of them could speak English. While none could, he found out that the prisoner San Diego had spent three years in the Mexican fishing fleet off of San Diego, California, and spoke a little Spanish. A couple of crew members from southern Texas could also speak a little Spanish and communicated with the other prisoners through the prisoner called San Diego.

After an initial period of uncertainty due to the Japanese prisoners onboard, the boat became more at ease and arranged themselves into a new routine. The prisoners were always under armed guard, but were given clean clothing, navy dungarees, and put to work performing menial tasks such as moving crates of food from the engine room bilges up to the crew's mess hall. In a bit of irony, the Gunner's

Mates and Torpedomen who were generally assigned as prisoner guards would often have them clean the submarine's weapons. Jones said, chuckling, "So here they're cleaning up one of the — I think it was a Browning Automatic or something, I don't remember what it was, and somebody said, 'Yeah, he's cleaning up the gun that shot him.' "[46] There were a few tense moments though, especially during gun actions, as Jones recalled:

> So when we sunk the second patrol vessel, you know, with 20 mm and 5-inch gun and all, you know it makes lots of noise down inside that steel hull. These three (prisoners) in the forward torpedo room was laying in their bunks. And when the guns started firing, they started jabbering in Japanese and jumping out of their bunks. And the guard pulled, he was a Torpedoman, pulled his 45 and cocked it and screamed at them, "Get back in your bunks!" So they knew what he said because they got back in their bunks.[47]

Other than this one incident related by Jones, humanity, respect, and kindness were shown to these men who were formerly enemies, subsequently prisoners, and ultimately comrades. As Jones succinctly put it, one of the favorite sayings about their enemy was, "That old Japanese rice farmer don't want this war any more than we do."[48] By the time the *Pogy* reached Pearl Harbor these men, American men and Japanese men, had found enough in common to form bonds of friendship:

> Well those prisoners we had, by the time we got them back to Pearl Harbor, three or four weeks later, you'd have thought they were members of the crew. They were playing grab-ass with the crew members. There was always a member present, they weren't playing grab-ass with the guard, but the others were very friendly.[49]

As the boat approached Pearl Harbor, the Captain made an announcement that concerned the Japanese prisoners. Jones related this announcement. "They have no money and no clothes." he [the Captain] said, "I'm depending on our crew correcting that."[50] And correct it they did. By the time that the Marines came onboard the *Pogy* to take charge of the prisoners, they were almost indistinguishable from the regular *Pogy* crew. Fresh haircuts, clean dungarees, and ample cash had all been supplied by their generous American shipmates. But the money was a problem, since if a Japanese prisoner was caught carrying American money, they would be severely punished; theft or looting of the dead would be assumed. Captain Ralph Metcalf had a stern talk with the commander of the Marine detail. Jones summarized the incident:

> So the skipper had the Marines come into the...stateroom. He said, "I want to talk to you people before you take custody of these prisoners." He said, "Now they do have American money on them. That American money was given to them by my crew." He says, "If I hear of anything happening to these prisoners," he says, "I'll certainly make it tough for you." And the Marines understood, I guess. He laid the law down to them.[51]

After this, his final war patrol, Jones was transferred to Submarine Relief Crew 281 and spent the remainder of 1944 and the beginning of 1945 on the West Coast, in Pearl Harbor, and on Guam onboard the submarine tender USS *Apollo* (AS 25). On March 29, 1945 he received orders transferring him back to New London, Connecticut, to instruct at the Submarine School. He had been promoted to Chief Petty Officer during his last run on the *Pogy* and was sitting at the bar in the Chief's Club on August 6 when the radio newsman announced that the United States had dropped the atomic bomb on Japan:

> And he was on the radio in the afternoon to bring the news, the newscaster. He started up, "Ladies and gentlemen, we just had a great thing happen," you know, something like that. But it caused everyone to straighten up from the bar to see what was happening, you know, the radio was up there. He said, "They just dropped — the United States just dropped a terrible bomb on Nagasaki, Japan.[52] One bomb destroyed the whole city." And boy, we all went, "Yay!" [Laughs] You know, even though I was back to teach school, inside there was a terrible fear that I might have to go back to the Pacific. Now I'd already spent about four years out there, except for the overhauls we had.[53]

Jones met his future wife, Veronica Barbara Sacharko, while stationed in New London, and they were married December 8, 1945. When his enlistment was up the next year, the young couple decided to make the navy their career. Chief Jones, his wife, and their growing family were transferred to several duty stations during his remaining years in the navy, including the USS *Sea Robin* (SS 407) in Panama, Naval Instructors' School in Great Lakes, Illinois, the USS *Tigrone* (SSR 419), and the Submarine Diesel School in New London, Connecticut.

Jones retired from the navy in 1956 and began work in the Piping Design Department at Electric Boat (EB) shipyards in Groton, Connecticut. He retired from EB in 1981 after twenty-five years and kept active with a real estate business, his children and grandchildren, and the companionship of his loving wife until her passing in 2009. He continues to live in the house they bought as newlyweds in East Lyme, Connecticut.

"I joined the navy for God, country and something to eat,"[54]

George Jones

USS *Pogy* (SS 266), c. 1944.
Courtesy SFM

CHAPTER 6

"THE FAITHFUL SHIPMATE"

Ernie Plantz with his sister Garnett at home in
West Virginia, c. 1941.
Courtesy Ernest V. Plantz

Name:	*Ernest "Ernie" V. Plantz*
Born:	*1920*
Joined Navy:	*July 1940*
Rating:	*Electrician's Mate*
Served On World War II	*USS Perch (SS 176)*
Submarines:	*Two War Patrols*
Service of Note:	*Prisoner of War: 1297 days;*
	March 3, 1942 to September 17, 1945
Left Service:	*Retired, November, 1970*

ERNIE PLANTZ WAS the faithful shipmate who spent 1297 days as a Japanese prisoner of war. A high school graduate in 1939, Plantz did not look forward to eking out a living on the family's "old boney farm" near Charleston, West Virginia, during a time when jobs were few and money was tight. His first move was into the Civilian Conservation Corps (CCC); the five dollars paid into his pocket and the ten dollars sent home to the family were welcome, but the CCC did not develop or fulfill Plantz's desire for a career, and Plantz had two desires for his future occupation; he wanted to be an electrician, and he wanted to join the navy. He remembered, "At any rate, I wanted to learn a trade. My parents were poor. I had no opportunity to go to college. And so the navy seemed like a good spot for me. They paid twenty-one dollars a month. That was apprentice seaman got twenty-one."[1]

For a boy from the landlocked state of West Virginia, a life at sea seemed at first to be an unusual choice, but the navy was somewhat of a family tradition. Plantz recalled, "I had a cousin that was in the navy, in submarines. And when he was on leave, he used to come visit with us..."[2] After receiving permission from his CCC commander, Plantz was off to boot camp in Norfolk, Virginia, and from there to his first duty station as an unrated seaman on the battleship USS *New Mexico* (BB 40), out in San Diego, California. Plantz tried unsuccessfully to move to the Engineering department and become a striker for the Electrician's Mate rating. Plantz was attracted to the work of the Electricians, knew that civilian electricians were always employed, and envied the Electricians on the battleship. "...most of them ran around changing light bulbs. I used to watch these Electricians run around in clean dungarees changing light bulbs in envy, you know?"[3] But no amount of trying could move Plantz into his desired rating onboard the *New Mexico*. There were other reasons for him to be dissatisfied, and one of the most important was food. The formality and rank structure on the surface ship kept Plantz hungry a good portion of the time. He explained:

> The food wasn't very good, it wasn't very plentiful. I, being one of the junior members of the crew, the way they arranged it, as a way of training you I guess, was you were seated at a table with [a] petty officer first class in charge of the table, and second class, and third class, and leading seamen, and then the most junior person sat at the far end of the table. Well the Mess Cook

went to the galley to get the food, they carried it back to the berthing space because that's where you ate. Then it started at the head of the table. The first class, they took what they wanted. It went down the line by the rates. When it got down to me, often times the tureen was empty. So the Cook had to rush back to the galley to see if he could get seconds. And if he did, instead of starting where they left off so I could get food, they started again at the head of the table. And sometimes, on seconds I didn't get any, either. And so it was, it wasn't happy.[4]

The *New Mexico* was sent to Bremerton, Washington, for a six-week overhaul that consisted mostly of work to clean, repair, and preserve the bottom of the ship. Members of the *New Mexico's* crew, including Plantz, primarily performed the cleaning, scraping, and wire-brushing on the underside of this enormous vessel. Overhaul completed, the battleship proceeded to Pearl Harbor, where Plantz made his final appeal for a transfer to Engineering and the Electrician's Mate rating and was again refused. Dejected, unhappy, and probably hungry, Plantz received a dinner invitation that changed the course of his navy life:

And then my cousin invited me over to his submarine, which was stationed in Pearl, on the *Plunger*, to have dinner with him, and after one dinner on that submarine I said, "Man, this is the place for me."[5]

It was April of 1941 when Plantz volunteered for submarine duty. At that time, the war in Europe was over a year old, and tensions were continuing to heat up in the Japanese sphere of influence. The United States was increasing its military presence in the Far East and this meant, among other things, adding another submarine squadron to the Asiatic Fleet stationed in Manila, Philippines. Plantz was assigned to the USS *Perch* (SS 176), a *Porpoise* Class fleet submarine stationed in Manila as a "direct input;" he was not required to first attend Sub School. He felt that this normal prerequisite was not required "…because they were desperate for people for submarines out on the old China Station in the Philippines."[6] Plantz had made the move from the formality of the battleship to the easy camaraderie of the submarine, but he still was not assured of a place in the Electrician's Mate ranks. He recalled how he "interviewed" for the position during his first days onboard the *Perch*:

> I checked aboard the submarine, and of course the COB is the first authority that you meet. He talked to me and wanted to know what I wanted to strike for. I told him I wanted to strike for Electrician. He said — well, he says, "Well I'll talk to the Engineer." And he did, and the Engineer cornered me then in the Control Room, introduced himself, and said, "I hear you want to be an Electrician." I said, "Yes sir." He says, "Well," he says, "are you a high school graduate?" And I said, "Yes sir." And then he says to me "Well," he says, "do you drink?" I didn't quite know how

USS *Perch* (SS 176), 19 November, 1936.
Courtesy SFM

to answer him. I says, "Yes sir, but I'm not very good at it." I says, "I'm getting better!" He looked at me just casually and said, "You'll do." That's how I got qualified to be an Electrician.[7]

Plantz, at last in the service he wanted, on the ship he wanted, doing the job he wanted, started down the path to acceptance as a fully qualified submariner and Electrician. But as was typical for new submarine crew members, that path was paved with dirty dishes; virtually everyone had to serve about the first three months onboard as Mess Cook. In addition to washing dirty dishes, pots, and pans, Mess Cooks would set and clear the tables, serve food from the galley during the meals, and help the Cooks break out stores in preparation for the next meal. It was hard, dirty, and tiring work that could put the sailor in a bit of a qualification "limbo." However, Plantz remembers using his mess cooking time to good advantage:

> Because mess cooking, if you used your time, you had a lot of time when you weren't doing mess cooking duties. So after the meal when you'd cleaned up, well, you had time, and if you were mess cooking you didn't have to stand any other watches. So I used the time to trace systems and make my drawings and get my notebook ready so I could qualify. I qualified [submarines] in July of '41...[8]

In addition to submarine qualification, Plantz was busy during these pre-war days on the *Perch* learning the duties of and qualifying as lookout when surfaced, and at the bow and stern planes station when submerged. Performing his duties as an apprentice Electrician could take him anywhere on the ship, whether it was watering and taking gravities on the batteries, repairing electrical equipment, or changing light bulbs. Plantz and the entire *Perch* crew also continually practiced the skills they would use in battle such as shooting torpedoes, making simulated runs on targets, and practicing crash dives. From the time Plantz reported aboard until the war started, the boat trained weekly, perhaps sensing that the first blow of war would come soon, but not knowing quite when or where.

As it turned out, Plantz and the *Perch* would have a ringside seat to the opening act of World War II in the Philippines. The *Perch* was anchored out in Manila Bay undergoing an engine overhaul on December 8 when the first Japanese attack came. Because of the extreme heat below decks in the boat, the cylinder heads had been removed and taken topside to grind valve seats and perform other needed maintenance in the shade of a temporary awning. The logistics of the disassembled engines put the *Perch* in a vulnerable position on the night of the attack. Plantz explained that as the Japanese attack began, "…it was a mad scramble to just get those parts back down below and start reassembling the engines, which they managed to do."[9] As the crew began the process of engine re-assembly, Japanese air attacks destroyed major portions of the Cavite Navy Yard, including their torpedo storage, repair facilities, and fuel oil storage tanks. The Japanese sank the first American submarine of the war, the USS *Sealion* (SS 195).[10] Helpless in the bay, the crew of the *Perch* could only watch as their duty station, their support services, and almost assuredly their comrades were annihilated. The Captain of the *Perch* gazed on the scene of destruction:

> …when they were bombing Cavite, they were blowing massive explosions. The Skipper was watching through the periscope in the Control Room, and he let some of us look through the scope at what was happening. I can remember him saying, "Good God, Van." Van Buskirk was our XO, he said, "Good God, Van, look at this." Things were really blowing. They knew exactly where things were at, they knew exactly what they wanted to hit, and they proceeded to do it.[11]

When again operational, the *Perch* made its way out of Manila Bay on December 10, was escorted through the minefield between the bay and Corregidor by an American patrol craft, and then slipped into the night and onto their first war patrol.

Leaving behind a burning confusion, they began their patrol off of northern Luzon with the orders to do what they could to impede the expected landing of the Japanese invasion force. When they had no luck making contact with enemy forces, they shifted their patrol area to the waters off Formosa, today known as Taiwan. After sinking one merchant vessel, the submarine was running low on torpedoes, food, and fuel oil, especially since their hasty departure from Manila allowed no time to top off these vital consumables. The *Perch* was ordered to Darwin, Australia, with a stop in Balikpapan in Borneo to load fuel oil for the diesel engines, literally days before the Japanese occupation of that island. The sub then proceeded through the Makassar Strait and arrived at Darwin, Australia. By that time the submarine tender USS *Holland* (AS 3), having also escaped from her Manila Bay station, arrived at Darwin and provided the means for the *Perch* to undergo a refit. Plantz and the *Perch* would remain in port for about two weeks while the boat was repaired, the sub was resupplied, and the crew's spirits were restored before leaving on their second and last war patrol.

The *Perch* was sent to the area around the Celebes Island, specifically, Kendari Bay, to observe and report on Japanese naval build-up in that area. After making their report, they were ordered to change their patrol station into the Java Sea, north of Java. However tempting the targets were in Kendari Bay, the shallow water inside this harbor would have necessitated a dangerous surface attack, so the *Perch* left this station and headed for Java. During their transit they came upon what appeared to be a single Japanese merchant ship. As they drew close to the merchant, a destroyer appeared from around behind and, as Plantz recalled, the destroyer:

> ...let go at us, put a five-inch shell right through the fairwater, just forward of the Conning Tower. It went right straight through it, it didn't explode, it just went through, thank the Lord. But it knocked out our radio transmitter because it ruptured the radio antennae trunk. And it knocked out our hydraulic oil accumulator tank, which at that point in time was topside, just forward of the Conning Tower. That was the real damage they did to us. We made, of course, an emergency dive and got the heck out of there...[12]

Proceeding on towards Java, the *Perch* encountered two Japanese destroyers on the night of March 1. The *Perch* dove, and the enemy destroyers passed without any action, but soon turned back, and one of them passed close enough to the sub's location for the Captain to consider a torpedo attack. At the last minute, the destroyer turned straight at the submarine. The attack was abruptly terminated, and the *Perch* headed deep to withstand a string of depth charges as the destroyer passed over. Heading for 180 feet, the *Perch* hit bottom at 147 feet.[13] She endured a depth charge attack, and the ship lost power on her port screw, but after the attack had ceased and the destroyers had moved away, the *Perch* was able to free herself from the bottom and return to the surface.

Just before dawn on March 2, two more Japanese destroyers were sighted, and again the *Perch* dove and headed for safety, only to stick firmly in the muddy bottom after descending to 200 feet. The destroyers were more persistent this time, though, and pounded the trapped submarine with depth charges for two days. Held captive by the destroyers and the suction of the muddy bottom, the *Perch* was methodically pummeled and experienced extensive injury, including damaged reduction gears, major electrical grounds, broken battery jars, and a major leak in the engine room hatch. The condition of the crew — at least the mental condition — also took a beating. In addition to the constant pounding of the exploding enemy depth charges, the condition of the air in the boat became almost unbreathable as oxygen was depleted and toxins accumulated. The pungency of the air was increased by the destruction of the porcelain toilets during the first attack and the requirement, as Plantz stated, of "going to the bathroom in a four-inch hole and no way to close it off."[14] The attack finally ended, as suggested by Lt. K. G. Schacht, a survivor of the *Perch*, because, "loss of air and oil during the attacks caused both previous enemy groups to believe their target had been destroyed."[15]

The destroyers ended their punishment on the evening of March 2, and the *Perch,* after an hour of agonizing attempts, finally broke free of the bottom and made it to the surface. Plantz recalled the emotions of that moment. "After about an hour, we broke through from the mud and started for the surface. Guys didn't look or act scared, you know, when we were trying to get out of the mud, but there sure was a sigh of relief when that darn hatch opened."[16] Though successful in reaching the blessed air, it was a mortally wounded submarine that floated on the exposed surface of the sea. Multiple hull leaks, ruptured air and ballast tanks, damaged electrical and propulsion systems, and questionable weapons systems made the *Perch* a vulnerable vessel unable even to effectively hide from her attackers. A test dive at dawn on March 3 revealed serious leaks in the conning tower hatch and the engine room hatch. The powerful and repeated blasts of the enemy depth charges had distorted the seating surfaces of these hatches to the point where they could no longer completely close. So damaged was the *Perch* and so severe and numerous were the leaks that even regaining the surface after the test dive was a battle for the crew. But their relief was short-lived. Plantz remembered:

So we had to emergency surface, and when we did, there was three Jap tin cans and two cruisers about three thousand, thirty-five hundred yards out ahead of us, and they started to fire. The first salvo went over us, the second one fell short of us, and the Skipper alerted us that we probably have to scuttle ship if we couldn't dive.[17]

Overmatched by the array of Japanese naval forces and unable to dive, Plantz and the *Perch* had few options. Even if the desire had been there, slugging it out with those five surface ships was not possible. As the official report described, "The submarine's [deck] gun was inoperative, and torpedoes could not be fired. Enemy depth charges had caused three of the *Perch's* torpedoes to run in their tubes, and the heat, exhaust gases, and nervous tension resulting therefrom [sic] had aggravated the already extremely difficult conditions."[18] The decision was made to abandon ship and to scuttle the boat. After fighting for days to keep the sea out, the crew began the disheartening process of opening valves to let in the seawater that would eventually flood the *Perch* and send her to the bottom. This gallant vessel was true to her nature even in her last dive. When discovered by Australian divers in 2007, the *Perch* was found on the bottom, intact, upright, and true, seemingly just resting on the ocean floor. As Plantz wistfully recalled, "Yeah, it was just a normal dive. Normal dive as it filled with water."[19]

The entire crew made it safely off of the *Perch* and were in the water for about an hour before being picked up and taken aboard one of the Japanese destroyers. The crew, now prisoners, were only kept on board a short time, but their valiant fight seemed to have gained the respect of their captors, according to Plantz. "So, we were on there until nightfall, on that destroyer, and then they transferred us, they were pretty good to us really. They gave us hard tack and some hot sake and water."[20] At the end of the day, Plantz and his shipmates were transferred to the *Op ten Noort*, a captured Dutch hospital ship that the Japanese were using as a floating prison.[21] Worthy opponents no more, the prisoners were treated more like livestock onboard the prison ship. The *Perch* crew members were placed in what was once a coal hold; this space contained no facilities or water and had a single entrance posted with an armed guard. They shared the space with the crews of British and Dutch ships that had been sunk off Singapore.

Conditions in the steaming hold, sealed, unventilated, and containing about fifteen hundred men, were abominable. Plantz recalled:

> Water was the real problem, because the source of water was top-side and the Japs wouldn't let you go up to get it. Finally they started letting one man at a time go to get water. Christ, we probably had fifteen hundred prisoners down in the hold, some of them badly burned and didn't get water for three or four days and no clothing to speak of, and third degree burns, their skin was just blisters; it was a horrible mess.[22]

The prisoners were fed only one time during the four-day trip to the location of the prison camp near the city of Makassar, on the island of Celebes. While in the water waiting to be picked up, the men of the *Perch* had actually joked about what they would be fed. Plantz recalled:

> Some of them were talking after we were still in the water after the ship had gone down. If the Japs — somebody asked, if the Japs pick us up, I wonder what they'll feed us? Somebody said, "Well, rice and fish, you idiot. What else do the Japs eat?" I piped up and said, "If it's rice, I hope it's with cream and sugar, because I can't eat plain rice." Three days later, when they finally gave you that first rice, God, it was better than any apple pie.[23]

The prisoners were offloaded and marched, many barefoot, through the streets of Makassar. This city is almost on the equator, and the blacktop streets were hot enough to burn, blister, and bleed, and their feet suffered in the column of marching men. Before heading for their final destination, the officers and certain key enlisted men, like the Radiomen, were removed and ultimately spent their imprisonment in camps on the home islands of Japan. The remaining enlisted men marched to a former Dutch army training camp that the Japanese had made into a detention facility for Allied prisoners. The *Perch* men were not the only Americans to be interned here. Survivors of the USS *Pope* (DD 225), a World War I-era four-stack destroyer, were also brought to the camp. The *Pope* had been sunk on March 1 as part of the same battle that claimed the *Perch*, a battle that was later called the Battle of the Java Sea. Very few light moments occurred during these early days of imprisonment, but Plantz did recall one:

Jake (Vandergriff) had the oldest pair of shoes. They were falling apart. His old steamers. And somebody says to him, "Mr. Vandergriff, why didn't you wear good shoes when you abandoned ship?" "Oh," he said, "I didn't want to get my good shoes wet."[24]

How does one go about describing such an experience? When privation, loss of liberty, starvation, disease, cruelty, and torture are the norm, then only experiences that significantly deviate from that norm are noteworthy. The prison camp experience for these sailors was one of the slow erosion of physical health and mental stability punctuated by moments of violence, brutality, and rarely, pleasure. The men who found themselves trapped in this nightmare kept alive and kept together because they kept the faith with each other. They made the best of it, bartered with the locals when they could, stole from the Japanese when the opportunities arose, and stayed true to their shipmates, their prison mates, and their country.

Because it was a preexisting facility pressed into a new use by the expediencies of war, the prison camp was well-built, with tile roofs and floors, good ventilation, and adequate facilities for housing, water supply, and sanitation. However, it became immediately obvious to Plantz that his captors were not going to expend many resources on providing food for their prisoners:

The food was, not much of it. The first months we were probably on Dutch stores that were captured. Bakery was a hamburger bun. Hamburger bun, that's what you got. And then they started giving us watery rice for breakfast and then in the evening, a small cup of rice. That went on for, I don't know, three or four months, and we finally convinced them that we had to have three meals a day, because that was what we were used to. So they started giving us another cup of rice at noon. It was just about a coffee cup of rice is what it was.[25]

The rice, according to Plantz, was the "worst and the oldest they could get" and contained more than just the rice; it contained rice worms. At first, the cooks would try to remove them from the rice before cooking, but their number made that impossible. The prisoners themselves would pick out the steamed carcasses from the rice, sometimes ending up with "half a cup of rice and a half a cup of worms." Finally, even that effort was abandoned. Plantz said, "So it didn't take long (until) we decided, hell, those worms are protein. We'll just ignore them and eat them along with the rice. You couldn't taste them."[26] Rarely, the prisoners were given dried fish to supplement their diet. Again, this menu item was not of the best quality nor very plentiful, and according to Plantz, it stunk:

...we used to call it stink fish because it did, it stunk, like fish. And that stuff had been sun dried, and flies had blown it. Before it had dried, they'd laid their eggs and the maggots, you know, were in the fish. You boiled it and just flicked the maggots out and eat the fish anyway.[27]

The inmates attempted to use their own ingenuity to supplement their diet, when occasion and opportunity allowed. On one occasion, a pet cat belonging to the Japanese Commodore meandered through the compound and ended up in the prisoner's stew pot. Surprisingly, there was no retaliation by their captors, perhaps because this incident occurred in the early days of camp operation. But as the rules and protocols became codified and understood, one of them concerning food was both ironic and maddening. Although the coconuts were so plentiful that they were almost bending down the trees, they were not to be harvested or eaten by the prisoners. Plantz and his shipmate, Turk Turner,[28] decided to risk the punishment and gather a few of the ripe nuts. Turner was the tree man; his job was to pick the fruit and toss it to Plantz waiting below. His job was just as important to the stealth, and therefore success, of the mission. "I had a rattan basket with a bail on it about the size of a bushel basket. And my job was to catch the nut, as it came down, in the basket and let it swing so it wouldn't make a thump when it hit the ground."[29] Plantz misjudged the descent of one errant nut, which struck and broke his wrist. In order to obtain permission to have the medical staff place a cast on his injured wrist, he fabricated a story for the Japanese master-at-arms that a carabao, or water buffalo, tethered and grazing nearby, had charged him, knocking him down and breaking his wrist. Before he got his cast the guard, "cussed me out a couple of times" and then told the doctor to set the wrist.

Apparently, providing the daily necessities for large groups of prisoner was far from the minds of the Japanese leadership as the war was waged in the Pacific. Plantz believed that the Japanese were caught off guard by the necessity to accommodate prisoners of war. In their military culture, surrender or allowing oneself to be captured was inconceivable; death was the preferable and honorable option. So the Japanese prison facilities all had an "ad hoc" nature, where the prisoners were tools of the Empire and deserving of minimal care only as long as they were useful in work and war production tasks. At first, the men were used for loading and offloading ships in the harbor of Makassar. For the most part, the tasks that the prisoners were

Makassar Prison Camp art; Men Pulling a Cart.
Drawing by Shorty Nagele, c. 1945.
Courtesy Ernest V. Plantz

given had some purpose, like cutting the lawns using strips of bamboo, salvaging construction materials from bombed-out buildings, or constructing defensive structures. However, the assignments were deliberately organized to be as difficult and erosive to the prisoners' physical condition as possible. One such tactic was to replace water buffalo with prisoners as the motive force to haul overloaded carts. Plantz had firsthand experience with these:

> And normally, why those two-wheeled carts were pulled by a water buffalo or a carabao, like we'd use oxen. They used a prisoner between the shafts and prisoners pushing this damn thing. I've seen guys drop dead pushing. They went on working party when they shouldn't have. They had malaria, you know, and malaria would go to their brain, and they would just, drop dead.[30]

Luckily for Plantz and the men of the *Perch*, they were spared being sent away in labor drafts. They remained in the camp near Makassar during their imprisonment and performed their work assignments in the immediate vicinity around the camp and city. The Japanese periodically took drafts of workers for labor assignments either off of the island or to work on important tasks on the island of Celebes. A draft of about two hundred men was conscripted for work in the mines near Kendari in eastern Celebes. A year later, less than one hundred returned, the balance dead from starvation, disease, and overwork.[31]

While most of the work assignments tended to slowly take their toll on the prisoners' health, others, especially the demolition work, could be immediately dangerous. Plantz recollected one such detail when an unstable wall collapsed and killed a sailor from the USS *Pope*. The Japanese reaction was unexpected and surprising to the rest of the prisoners:

> ... the Japs treated him with a regular military funeral with an American flag, and he laid in state, and the damn Jap admiral come and paid his respects and bowed and treated him just like he was one of their own people because he had died working for the Emperor. That's the difference in them.[32]

That was the only instance that occurred when the prisoners were treated as men worthy of respect. Usually, the Japanese guards, considering the prisoners as something less than human, relied on violence, cruelty, and a baseball bat to communicate their intentions. Absent a common language, prisoners discovered where the "boundaries" were by seeing when a beating would occur. Incidents that occasioned the use of the bat for a beating allowed the prisoners to develop a mental rule book about what was allowed and what was forbidden. The guards showed little humanity toward the prisoners, Plantz said:

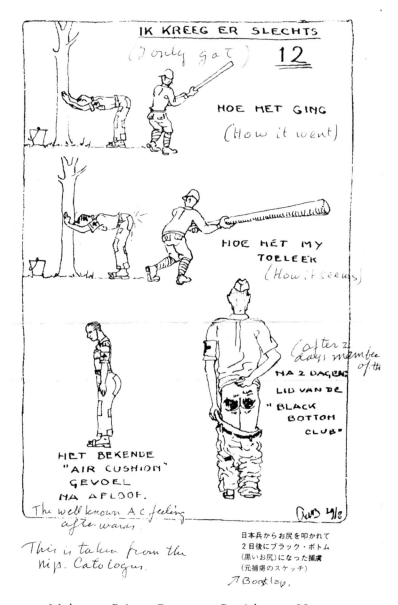

Makassar Prison Camp art; Punishment Humor.
Drawing by Dr. A.J.P. Borstlap, c. 1945.
Courtesy Ernest V. Plantz

... they were very cruel, most of them. They didn't give a hoot whether you lived or died. They hoped you died. They'd beat you for little or no reason at all just because they could or because you did something they didn't want you to do, but you didn't know that they didn't want you to do it. That's the way you found the rules. Somebody would do something, and they'd beat them.[33]

Plantz himself recalled receiving a particularly memorable beating when a guard struck him seventy-five times on the backside before he mercifully passed out. The extensive damage to blood vessels, and sometimes bones, and the always extensive bruising caused recipients of such punishment to be initiated into the informal "black bottom club." What was Plantz's offense that deserved being beaten unconscious? This starving man was trading with natives for food.[34]

Rarely, a work assignment would have a pleasant or humorous aspect. Once, while building an underground radio station for the Japanese, Plantz was assigned to help reassemble a radio tower that had been transported from another location. As a young man unafraid of heights, he remembered a moment or two of relaxation at the top of the tower. "I liked it up there. The Japs couldn't get at me, and I had a good view."[35] On another occasion one of Plantz's shipmates off the *Perch*, GM3 Earl R. Harper[36], complied maliciously with a guard's orders, with humorous results:

The warrant officer [Japanese] in charge, he wanted to take a hot bath. They liked — like I guess, a sauna or like that, homemade. And they heated it with an outside fire. And he was inside this bamboo hut. And he kept hollering. He had a prisoner feeding the doggone fire, and he kept hollering at him to make it hotter. So Earl Harper poured the wood onto the dang thing and all at once it was, kind of like I guess, a frog in a kettle; he was cooking him alive. And it's kind of the way the water got. Burned the Jap, he hopped out and then was chasing the guard for making his water too hot.[37]

Plantz believed that the Japanese authorities treated the prisoners so inhumanely because they were able to dehumanize these prisoners since they had disgraced themselves, "by choosing to be captured instead of dying. They thought your parents would disown you and your government; it would be a disgrace with them. So they figured they could treat us anyway they wanted to and nobody would care."[38] In a disturbing parallel to the attitude of the Nazis toward their Jewish citizens and prisoners, these POWs were referred to by the Imperial Japanese military as "The Problem." The prisoners, no longer fellow humans but now just an abstract "Problem," could be treated as objects, or at best, as useful machines.

Plantz had been in prison for more than a year when the prison officials decided that the former Dutch army camp would be more useful as a training camp for Indonesian recruits fighting on the side of the Japanese. The inmates were directed to build a new camp for themselves using locally available materials. The location they chose would be a new source of hardship and mortality for the prisoners of war. Plantz remembered:

> So they had us clear and build a bamboo camp, about a mile south from where we were at. Unfortunately, they chose an area that was wet in the rainy season. The Dutch had always quarantined it because of the presence of malaria and dysentery, and that's where they built our camp. The winter, the rainy season, of '44, '45, that's when most of our people died. Anyway, it was pretty rough, because during the rainy season the water would stand in some of the barracks a foot deep. You slept on boards that were up on a rack. That was a beautiful breeding place for mosquitoes. The septic tank and the well were too close together, and in higher water it contaminated the water. So guys would get dysentery and malaria, and they'd die of dysentery and malaria and starvation.[39]

Plantz learned firsthand of the disease-rife nature of the new camp when he contracted first dysentery and then malaria in January of 1945. Having lived almost three years on a scarcely subsistence diet, his body had few resources to draw on when these twin maladies struck. Weighing one hundred and seventy-five pounds at the time of his capture, Plantz had wasted away to a mere one hundred pounds when he got sick. He remembered, "I just slowly lost weight, you know, over three and a half years. Then when I got sick, there was nothing to fall back on. I remember I could reach around my damn leg with one hand."[40]

His physical crisis came as he attempted to get to the latrine. "The last thing I remember, I was crawling from the barracks to the bathroom and evidently passed out before I got to the bathroom. And when I woke up, it was six days later in a hospital, makeshift camp hospital."[41] That Plantz woke up at all was due to the heroic efforts of a Dutch doctor and fellow prisoner in the Makassar camp. Using what could be improvised, recycled, or stolen, the doctor had crushed quinine tablets, mixed them with fermented coconut juice, and injected this concoction into Plantz's arm using a homemade syringe. Plantz recovered thanks to this improbable remedy but by the end of the ordeal he believes his weight had dropped to seventy-five or eighty pounds. However, he was one of the lucky ones, as he remembers that during this period inmates died at the rate of "anywhere from six to ten or twelve a day in the camp."[42]

Enduring such conditions, it would seem that escape would be the first priority; but escape to where? The *Perch* crew knew that there had been no opportunity to send a message about the scuttling of their boat due to the damaged radio transmitter. Also, they were not entirely sure where the camp was located, and the loyalties of the locals around the camp were uncertain. Three Dutch sailors found this out the hard way:

> ... three guys attempted to escape. The Indonesians turned them in to the Japs, and the Japs captured them and brought them back, beat hell out of them for a week, took them out, made them dig their own graves, and chopped their heads off. And they told us that if anyone escaped or if anyone attempted to escape, that they'd probably chop off their heads, and they'd chop off ten of their friends or if you didn't have any friends, ten of the people that slept closest to you. That's why there weren't any more escapes or attempted escapes.[43]

As it turned out, these men had entrusted a local native ruler who promised to provide a boat and a crew to take them to Australia. The native ruler took their money and turned them in to the Japanese authorities and was rewarded for his duplicity. When the men got to the boat, Japanese soldiers were inside the boat waiting for them.

Starvation, hard labor, and physical abuse were the main tools the Japanese prison guards used to manage their charges, but they occasionally employed more subtle tools. Members of the Kempeitai, the Japanese military police, were assigned to the Makassar camp. Sometimes called the "Japanese Gestapo" in Allied propaganda, this branch of the Imperial Japanese Army provided regular law enforcement duties but also supplied personnel for running prisoner of war, forced labor, and special camps. The Kempeitai officer at Makassar acted much like a secret police or political officer when he probed for ideological weakness in the ranks of the prisoners and attempted to exploit it for intelligence or propaganda value. The target of one of his forays was a member of the *Perch* crew, a Filipino cook named Sarmiento, nicknamed Ping[44]. He was probably targeted due to the superficial dissimilarity of this sailor from the rest of the *Perch* crew; his skin was dark, and he was one of the older men. Plantz recalled the one time when the Japanese political officer tried to recruit Sarmiento:

> Anyway he [the Kempeitai] says, "You don't like the Americans, do you?" Ping says, "Well, I don't know." He says, "I haven't made up my mind. I've only been in the navy twenty-seven years." Then he [the Kempeitai] says, "Well, you know if you help me," he says, "I'm in a position to help you." He says, "You have a family in Manila, do you?" "Oh yes." He says, "Well, if anything happened to you, why, who'd take care of them?" "Oh," he said, "if anything happened to me" he said, "she'd be a rich widow." He said, "I've got insurance with Uncle Sam, $10,000." That was old Ping. He was a great guy.[45]

The furious and frustrated Kempeitai officer left empty-handed. According to Plantz, no one ever cooperated with these attempts to exchange information for special favors. Sometime later, and seemingly on a different tact, the Kempeitai approached the entire crew with an offer of taking them on a fishing trip. When asked if they liked to fish someone on the crew replied, "Sure, who doesn't? We're Americans." Promising to try to arrange an excursion some Sunday, the officer left, and the men of the *Perch* promptly forgot about it. However, the following Sunday, Japanese guards with shovels, burlap bags, and rattan baskets collected the crew and marched them off to their fishing trip. Instead of heading for the ocean or a lake, the party, with their unusual fishing gear, marched to an abandoned fish hatchery.

The hatchery ponds were about a half acre in size and still contained many fish. The prisoners were ordered to divide one of these ponds down the middle by building an earthen wall, bail the water from one side to the other, and then collect the stranded fish. The intense heat, fetid water, and stinking mud slowed the agonizing project. The pace didn't satisfy the angry Kempeitai officer, remembered Plantz:

> So we went to work bailing the water and building the dam and weren't working fast enough for the Japs. They'd come along and whack you on the back with a piece of bamboo, to work harder. And this doggone Kempeitai spoke English, he's standing there on the bank watching. He says, "You wanted to go fishing?" He says, "Now fish you bunch of bastards!"[46]

Once the pond had been drained and the fish had been collected, the Japanese guards took the larger fish and allowed the prisoners to have the smaller ones. But when the prisoners boiled the little fish, they gave off such a foul stench, not even the starving men could eat them. Apparently, though, the Japanese ate their fish and all came down with a terrible case of what Plantz called, "the squirts." "So we got the last laugh on them." Plantz said, "That was a good fishing party, because it made them sick, because they ate theirs."[47]

Hard labor, little food, and insufficient medical care were the routine as the years rolled by. Only the faithfulness and support of this group of shipmates for each other kept them together. The men naturally divided in smaller cooperative, but not competitive, groups, usually centered on one's bunking location. Extra food and resources were pooled and shared among the group members. One unusual item that was carefully collected and shared was eggshells. Though uncertain exactly where the idea came from, Plantz recalled that they would grind up eggshells and add them to their rice as a food supplement. Due to the introduction of the calcium from the eggshells, he believed this practice to be responsible for the American prisoners surviving their experience with their teeth, their bones, and their posture still intact.[48]

Then one day, a day like any other of the one thousand, two hundred and ninety-seven days that had preceded it, the prisoners were called to assembly by the Japanese guards. Plantz recalled the joy and the irony of that day:

They called us together and announced to us that the war was over and that the Americans had won. And they wanted to shake hands, "Now we're friends." These were the same bastards that beat you and starved you for three and a half years, because we kept the same guards from beginning to end. They wanted to shake hands and be friends. Needless to say, nobody did.[49]

Plantz and the men would spend another month in the camp due in part the logistics of removing the remaining number of prisoners from the remote island, but initially because nobody knew they were there. Absent the report or confirmation from another Allied ship, the *Perch* had been assumed lost with all hands back in 1942. The families of the crew men had all been informed that their sons were "missing and presumed dead" and had mostly made their peace with this news. However, Ernie Plantz's own mother told him she never gave up hope and always was convinced that her son was alive and would eventually return home. An apprentice Radioman among the prisoners was able to gather an old radio and spare parts and cobble together a transmitter. Once the Allied forces became aware of the survivors of the Makassar prison camp, it would still be another month before they could identify, medically stabilize, and evacuate the freed inmates, first to Borneo, then, for Plantz, back to Hawaii and eventually to a hospital facility near San Francisco.

Of the over three thousand men initially imprisoned at the Makassar camp, only about a thousand remained when the war ended. While much of the decrease was due to prisoner transfers to other Japanese work projects, hundreds had died due to the twin killers of starvation and disease. The crew of the *Perch* made out quite well, losing only six shipmates during their incarceration out of a crew of fifty-nine. Plantz attributes this to a tougher American constitution, as he recalled that the English and Dutch prisoners died at a higher rate, something closer to thirty percent. This was especially true of the English "boy sailors." Boys as young as twelve were allowed to serve in a limited capacity on British ships in the hopes of gaining a good position in a naval career. Plantz looked back upon the occasions of their passing with melancholy:

We had a number of them [boy sailors] that were prisoners that had been on the English battleship *Prince of Wales* in particular.

And they'd get sick and when [those] guys were dying they'd lay there all night long crying for their mother. Broke your heart. [50]

Plantz spent the first few weeks after his return to the States in the Oak Knoll Naval Hospital in San Francisco undergoing rehabilitation and medical observation. Most of his time was his own, for rest and recuperation, so he and his buddies would try to make up for lost time. One of their early expeditions was an attempt to walk the fifteen miles from the hospital to downtown San Francisco. Just walking the distance was too dull for these entertainment-starved men, so Plantz and his three *Perch* shipmates, EM2 J.H. "Jesse" Robison, EM2 A.W. Winger, and EM2 M.M. "Turk" Turner found a way to make it more interesting. "We would stop at each bar along the way and have one drink. We tried for three or four days. We never did get to San Francisco, but we sure did get drunk."[51] Each time he would return to the hospital, there'd be a message to call Operator 5 in Athens, Ohio. Plantz discounted these messages as some navy error, since he didn't know anyone in Athens, Ohio. Unbeknownst to him, the Plantz family had moved into the Athens area during the three and a half years of his imprisonment. He happened to travel through there on his way to West Virginia, where he assumed his family was still living. During his train stop in Athens there, he remembered the repeated messages from Operator 5 and called her on a lark. That call set off a frantic search for the Plantz family. The son was reunited with his family, proving that Mrs. Plantz had been right all along; her boy was alive.

Plantz did eventually pay a visit to his original hometown in South Charleston, West Virginia. He was amused to see his name listed among the dead on the war memorial. He visited his high school and was invited to speak at their assembly. But he wanted to see one of his favorite teachers, Mr. Poe, a science teacher, who had been promoted to principal of the junior high school in the city. Plantz went unannounced to the junior high and shocked his former teacher:

So I walked in to see him, and he looked at me, and he turned just as white as a doggone sheet. He says, "Ernie Plantz, you're dead. What are you doing here?" I says, "They forgot to tell me."[52]

After completing his recuperation, Plantz was assigned to the reserve submarine, the USS *Tautog* (SS 199). The submarine, originally in Portsmouth, New Hampshire, was put in Reserve Commission and towed from Portsmouth down to New Orleans, transported up the river and through the canals to Chicago, and towed across Lake Michigan to a berth in downtown Milwaukee. Plantz was stationed there for two years as ship's keeper and instructor to the reserve students. For Plantz, this duty was the perfect assignment:

> That was good duty. It was also the best duty I ever, I could have possibly had after the war because I went from Second Class to Chief, you know, when I went back to duty. I sure as hell didn't know what a Chief Electrician's supposed to know. I don't think I remembered the submarine quite as well as I should have. So by teaching the reserves gave me a good opportunity to learn what I didn't know, or re-learn. So it helped a heck of a lot when I went to an operating boat.[53]

Plantz remained in the navy and served in a number of submarines after the war, but he did his best to keep the past in the past. As he said, "Very few in the navy knew I was a prisoner, former prisoner, because I didn't tell them. I wanted to make my own way on my own efforts. I didn't want any sympathy."[54] He became a Chief Electrician and eventually made the transition to the officer ranks, retiring as a Lieutenant in 1970. Plantz made his home and raised a family in Ledyard, Connecticut.

In 1997, Plantz made a trip to the site of the prison camp where he spent three and half years of his youth. "Difficult in a way, I guess, but it freed me up a little bit." He also began going to Post Traumatic Stress Disorder (PTSD) meetings only a few years ago. His wife Caroline felt, "That really helped a lot. He started talking freely about it [his experiences as a prisoner], because he never talked about it when the kids were growing up. They knew he was a POW, but they didn't know any of the specifics. And really, the whole experience influenced him a lot." [55]

Plantz spent the years after the navy in public service including ten years on the Ledyard Connecticut Zoning Board, serving for four of those years as its chairman. He is a long-time member of the Ledyard Lions Club and received the Melvin Jones award, the organization's highest form of acknowledgement of an individual's dedication to humanitarian service. Plantz also remains an active member of the Submarine Veterans of World War II, Thames Chapter, and is generous with his time for those interested in hearing of his experiences. He was inducted in 2005 into the Connecticut Veterans Hall of Fame by Connecticut Governor Jody Rell and received a belated Bronze Star in 1997 for his service and sacrifice; recognition, and honor long overdue for this faithful shipmate.

"I was a little bit ashamed of how I spent the war because my shipmates died and I lived. I lived because I helped the Japs. They died because they were fighting the Japs. That's enough to make you feel guilty."[56]

Ernie Plantz

Plantz topside on USS *Tautog* (SS 199) in Milwaukee WI, c. 1946.
Courtesy Ernest V. Plantz

CHAPTER 7

"THE WILLING WARRIOR"

Jeweldeen Brown underway on the deck of the
USS *Trout* (SS 202), c. 1942.
Courtesy Jeweldeen Brown

Name:	*Jeweldeen "Deen" Brown*
Born:	*1922*
Joined Navy:	*March, 1941*
Rating:	*Radioman*
Served On World War II	*USS Trout (SS 202)*
Submarines:	*Eight War Patrols*
	USS Gar (SS 206)
	One War Patrol
Service of Note:	*Doolittle Raid on Tokyo,*
	Battle of Midway,
	Solomon Islands, & Peleliu /
	Palau Battles
Left Service:	*Retired, 1963*

DEEN BROWN WAS the willing warrior who, though he ultimately made a career of the navy, joined the service as an answer to his country's call in her time of need. He didn't join the navy with the intention of becoming a submariner, but as he learned more about America's undersea fleet, he moved deliberately from battleship sailor, to submarine support worker, and eventually to qualified submariner and senior Radioman on a World War II fleet boat. His navy career began in the small town of Rockville, Missouri, about as far away from the ocean as one can get. Europe was embroiled in war in early 1941, and America was gearing up for the hostilities sure to come, when Brown decided to join the navy. Not wanting to risk being drafted by the army and attracted by the navy's training and education programs, "I went to Kansas City, and in March of 1941, and I joined the navy."[1] He was immediately sent to San Diego, California, for basic training. After completing boot camp, he received his assignment to the battleship USS *Nevada* (BB 36), with an approved delay to allow him to attend Radioman Training School, also in San Diego. During America's build-up to war, men who had the aptitude to fill the Radioman rating, or other technical specialties such as Electrician's Mate and Machinist's Mate, were in high demand. The number of men qualified to perform the work of these ratings was adequate for peacetime but was severely understaffed for the task of war.

Brown was selected for Radio School, and it was there that he first met men of the submarine navy, of which he said, "...I was impressed with them because they all seemed to be a lot smarter than I was. So they were breezing through the course that I was struggling to make a 3.5. So I thought, my, those guys are okay. Maybe that would be a good outfit to get into. It was in the back of my mind, you know."[2] One of his instructors, a Radioman Chief, also encouraged him to volunteer for submarines, commenting that he would learn at lot about his rating onboard the boats. For Brown, whose prime motivation for choosing the navy over the other services was its opportunities for education and instruction; this was just the right thing to say.

After graduating from the Radio School, Brown awaited transportation to the *Nevada*, in Pearl Harbor. While waiting, he was assigned to a temporary job at the navy radio station in San Diego that was also home to a squadron of the older S-class submarines. The station's lack of an operational mess hall drove the young Brown down to the submarine docks to renew old Radio School friendships and to scrounge food. What he found onboard these boats only intensified his attraction to the submarine service and made him sure that, as soon as his new command would allow, he would apply for a transfer to the boats. His initial trips to these submarines were primarily motivated by his hunger. As Brown stated:

> But I found out that the guys on the S-boats had food all the time. And most of the time, they ate very good, you know, so as soon as I found that out, I'd go down to the S-boats, visit with those guys, and eat whatever they had to eat, and, yeah, so I spent quite a lot of time talking with them.[3]

But his attraction was driven by more than just hunger. Brown stated that, "...I was rather intrigued with the complexity, and I was somewhat awed that these guys could learn to operate that thing." He was also impressed by, "You know, instruments everywhere, all of that, of course, was mysterious to me. And so I was somewhat awed by that, and I thought ... just to learn how to operate this thing would be an education in itself."[4]

About a week after the Japanese attack, Seaman First Class Brown arrived in Pearl Harbor on a navy transport ship, and the first thing he saw was his first duty station, the battleship USS *Nevada*. What should have been a moment of excitement and pride was instead one of horror and dismay because, as Brown related, "The very first ship you could see as you entered the harbor was, in fact, the *Nevada*. It was sitting there aground with decks awash. I looked at that, and I recognized it immediately because the superstructure was a bit unique, and I knew it was my ship."[5] Though more than a week had passed since the December 7th attack, the harbor was still a scene of destruction, confusion, and chaos. The harbor was covered in oil, some fires were still burning, and divers worked to recover bodies from the sunken warships. With his ship on the bottom, Brown realized that "...I also had to find a new home, I wasn't going to get on that one." His efforts to find the officers of the *Nevada* failing, he made his way to the receiving station, somewhat of a holding area for waiting or unassigned sailors. For the officer in charge of the receiving station, Brown was just another headache in an endless string of headaches.

Unshaven, irritable, and exhausted, the officer knew Brown couldn't report to the *Nevada* but had no alternative idea until Brown suggested that he'd like to go to the submarine base. According to Brown, the officer looked at him and said, "Goodbye and good luck."[6]

Brown walked the two miles from the receiving station to the entrance of the submarine base, carrying his sea bag. He was stopped at the entrance to the base until it was discovered he was a Radioman. Transformed from vagrant to VIP, a jeep materialized for Brown that whisked him through personnel in-processing to the mess hall for a quick meal and finally to the Pearl Harbor sub base radio station. Brown was immediately put to work. "I went on watch there on a radio circuit. We were handling an awful lot of traffic to the United States. A lot of it was personnel information trying to answer queries about sailors who had been there and were missing and so forth."[7] On watch at the radio station his first hectic day, Brown worked the circuit from about 7 o'clock in the evening until about 1 or 2 o'clock in the morning. When he asked his supervisor for permission to go to the barracks for some rest, the supervisor refused. He said, "No. You go outside, you'll get shot." Still fearful of a Japanese invasion, sentries of all services patrolled the island and, "Some of them were a little trigger-happy. And some of them were shooting first and asking questions later."[8] Once the sun was up, Brown was able to find a place in the barracks, unpack his sea bag, and officially complete his first day on Pearl Harbor.

Doing an important job at a crucial time, Brown remained in the radio station for almost four weeks, handling radio traffic for the Submarine Base, Commander in Chief – Pacific Fleet (CINCPAC), and other navy commands. The pace was demanding, and the hours were long during these opening days of war for America. The endless message traffic sometimes became personal for Brown, as he sometimes had to transmit lists of the confirmed dead from the Japanese attack. "I would see either one of my classmates or one of my boot camp mates, people that I knew. And, of course, that was saddening, but I had to do my job and keep going."[9]

Not content with being close to the submarines but not on them, Brown's gentle lobbying of his personnel officer finally landed him a position on the submarine support tender, USS *Pelias* (AS 14). As a member of a submarine relief crew on the *Pelias*, Brown, promoted to Radioman Third Class, worked on submarines that returned from war patrols. A war patrol on a fleet submarine was so arduous that the boat's crew, on their return from sea, was given up to a month rest and relaxation (R&R). A tender, like the *Pelias*, placed a relief crew onboard to conduct repairs, replenish supplies, and stand any necessary watches. When the regular crew returned, their boat was ready to return to sea, tanks filled, weapons loaded, and battle damage repaired. Brown, as a Radioman on a relief crew, would repair any damaged electronic equipment onboard, perform necessary maintenance, and assist in the installation of new equipment.

Pelias was the tender for Submarine Squadron Six, which consisted of all brand new boats. These boats were of the *Tambor* (*Thresher, Triton, Trout*, etc.) class, their names all began with the letter T, and the *Gar* class boats (*Grayback, Grenadier, Gudgeon*, etc.).[10] Brown did some relief crew work on many of these boats, notably an electronic equipment overhaul on the *Tuna* and some routine electrical maintenance on the *Trout*. These jobs were vital to the operation of the submarine fleet and an essential contribution to the war effort. But working on a submarine was not the same as being part of a submarine crew, and it was not enough for Petty Officer Brown. The *Trout* was scheduled to mount a relief effort for the stranded American military on the island of Corregidor in the Philippines. Brown helped load the *Trout* with ammunition for the soldiers and sailors on the island and approached the Executive Officer with a request to join the relief effort and the crew. His request was denied, but he got a promise that when they returned, if he was still in the relief crew, he would be taken aboard.

The Exec was as good as his word, and Brown became a member of the crew of the USS *Trout* (SS 202). However, in order to make room for himself and the other implements of war, he first assisted the crew in unloading twenty tons of gold and silver, the entire treasury of the government of the Philippines, which had been removed from the island to avoid its capture by the Japanese.[11] Reports document that once the *Trout* unloaded the ammunition at Corregidor, she was underballasted, having left most of her torpedoes in Pearl to make room for the ammunition. When the Captain requested several tons of sand or gravel in sandbags, he was told that that was the one commodity the defenders of the island could not spare. Would he take instead an equal weight of gold and silver as ballast? Thus, the treasury of the Philippine government was rescued, the *Trout* sailed smoothly home, with a brief detour to sink an enemy ship along the way, and Radioman Brown helped unload his new boat, which came to be nicknamed the "gold" ship.[12]

Brown, with a little luck and a lot of smarts, had managed to maneuver himself onto a fleet submarine while bypassing many of the steps a regular submarine sailor would have taken. The usual path to submarines involved passing through the Submarine School in New London, Connecticut. As a Radioman originally destined for the surface fleet, Brown had never been to Sub School. When he reported onboard the *Trout*, they knew he had not had the benefit of submarine training but still gave him an ultimatum. The Executive Officer told Brown, "Well, we're going to give you six months. You have to qualify in six months, or you're gone." Brown qualified in four months. Humble about this remarkable achievement he explained, "Well, I couldn't go anywhere, there was no liberty. So all I had to do in my spare time was study the boat, and make diagrams and so forth."[13]

Brown had effectively transferred himself from the surface fleet to the submarine service, landed a shore job as a radio operator on the Submarine Base, maneuvered himself onto the Squadron Six submarine tender USS *Pelias*, and then talked himself onto the *Trout*. What drove someone like Brown to continue to strive for a front-line assignment when any of the previous navy positions he held were safer, valuable, and honorable assignments? According to Brown, "I wanted to get on a submarine. I really — I wanted to get the experience, and I wanted to be a qualified submariner." This type of desire to be a member of this elite organization, regardless of the danger, was not unique to Brown. Once in the submarine service, the ultimate goal of the men was most often to get assigned to a boat.

Sometimes this desire led the men to go to extreme measures. One such man was Joe "Stowaway" Holmes, a retired Chief Torpedoman, who passed away in 2006 at the age of eighty-two. During the war, Holmes was assigned to a submarine relief crew on Midway Island. Unable to find an open billet on one of the boats through conventional means, Holmes "hitched a ride" onboard the USS *Flasher* (SS 249), hiding in the bilges until he thought that the boat was too far from land to return. Once this point was reached, Holmes "appeared" from the bilges, reported for duty to the Captain, became part of the crew, and earned the nickname "Stowaway."[14] Brown

USS *Trout*: unloading the Philippine gold, c. March, 1942.
Courtesy SFM

spoke for most of the sailors like himself and "Stowaway" when he explained why the danger of front-line duty was not a major concern for him when he said, "I was young, and like most young people, I was invincible."[15]

But even with the increased danger of being a member of a submarine crew aside, to exchange the relatively lush personal comforts of a battleship billet for the extremely Spartan accommodations onboard a submarine seems ludicrous. The fleet submarines had very little crew space, cramped working areas, and mostly non-existent hygiene facilities. Showers were routinely secured during a patrol as the batteries and food service need prevailed. Brown clearly explained one of the main motivations that drew sailors from the surface to the submarine navy:

> One thing I liked about the submarine navy was, number one, it was not spit and polish regulation. Like [in] the battleship navy, sailors will spend half the day shining brightwork so the Captain's railings on his ladders would look good or something like that. That — to me, that was an awful waste of manpower. Submarine guys had something real to do. Meaningful. And that's what meant a lot to me; I wanted to do something meaningful and real. Never mind the spit and polish.[16]

Brown's first two war patrols, the *Trout's* third and fourth, were right out of the front pages of the war news of the day. In April of 1942, the *Trout,* with her sister boat, the *Thresher,* provided forward intelligence and weather reports for Admiral Halsey in support of what is known as the Doolittle Raid on the Japanese homeland. Navy Task Force 16 and 18, including the USS *Hornet* and *Enterprise,* mounted this morale-building raid on Tokyo in part to retaliate for the sneak attack on Pearl Harbor and also to boost the morale on the home front, recently depressed by a string of Japanese victories.[17] The two submarines involved in this mission were to take position at the mouths of Tokyo (*Thresher*) and Kobe (*Trout*) harbors and report only if they observed the Japanese fleet leaving the harbor en masse, an indication that the secret mission had been discovered. Additionally, they were to report if the weather conditions would prevent visual bombing, since the B-25 bombers were not permitted to carry the top secret Norden bombsights with them when overflying Japanese controlled territory.

Radioman Brown may have been the first person in the Allied fleet to become aware of the raid's effectiveness. Brown was monitoring a Tokyo radio broadcast, even though it was in Japanese, until, "… on this one particular morning, this radio station went off the air abruptly. I thought, that's strange. You know, they didn't normally do that. Well it wasn't very long after that until we were informed that the bombers had been launched. Then I knew why the radio station went off the air.

The bombing had started taking place."[18] So secret was the *Trout's* mission that even in the war patrol report, written after the fact, the destination of the *Trout* was designated "Area _____."[19]

The *Trout's* fourth war patrol was a mission in support of the Battle of Midway. Before this patrol, she had returned to Pearl Harbor for a repair period to overhaul the four engines and replace their "dry" mufflers with "wet" mufflers. This was a serious concern, since the dry mufflers allowed "sparking of the engines," as was noted in the Captain's war patrol report from the Doolittle Raid.[20] These sparks, generated by the running engines, especially during power changes, would "light-up" the position of a surfaced submarine at night, definitely not a desirable war-time feature. When these repairs and improvements were only partially completed, the *Trout* received orders to leave immediately and begin support of what would become the Battle of Midway. The *Trout* put to sea twenty-four hours later, after a Herculean effort by shipyard workers and crew to make her seaworthy, but with only a single operational main engine. The rest of the repair work was completed at sea. Brown remembered:

> I'll tell you, there must have been a hundred and fifty shipyard workers on that damn ship. We got underway on one engine, one main engine. And all hands turned-to and helped the enginemen and we actually finished assembling those engines underway. That was really risky business.[21]

The navy submarines, including the *Trout*, formed a protective ring to attempt to prevent a Japanese amphibious landing on Midway. Due to the effectiveness of the carrier battle against the Imperial Japanese fleet, this landing never materialized. Unable to participate in the military action, *Trout* contributed to the battle by picking up several Japanese sailors from the Imperial Japanese Navy's heavy cruiser, *Mikuma*, and returned them to Pearl Harbor for interrogation. When Brown related this story in an article for *Polaris*, the magazine of the Submarine Veterans of World War II, he described a surprisingly gentle treatment for these rescued sailors. "We took them aboard, cleaned a thick layer of black oil from their bodies and tendered them with juice and water"[22], he wrote. The younger of the two prisoners was described as friendly and talkative, while the older was silent. Brown believed that the older man was adhering to some code of honor, but once examined at Pearl Harbor, the prisoner was discovered to have broken seven ribs during his escape from his sinking ship. Breathing was probably painful for him, and talking would have been agony.

Though a war patrol on a World War II vintage submarine has been compared to living for two months in your basement, submariners like Brown did find ways to entertain themselves during idle hours. [23] Though card games like cribbage and poker were played throughout the fleet, the poker games held on the *Trout* after the boat was home ported out of the Australia became a bit more serious. Brown explained:

> And especially when we were operating out of Australia, sometimes they'd be a lot of money in a poker game. The reason for that is because a pound note — Australia had the English money system, and a one pound note was worth three dollars and twenty five cents. But you get these guys in a poker game, and they start playing these one pound notes like they were one dollar bills. So, I've seen lots of poker games in the mess hall that probably had way more than a thousand dollars in it.[24]

Movies were also shown in the Forward Torpedo Room and those, along with records, were traded among the other boats and with the submarine tender. In his report after the *Trout's* second war patrol, the Captain, Lieutenant Commander Frank Wesley Fenno, Jr., noted, "Record players bought prior to this patrol proved to be the best single items of amusement for the crew; but the greatest morale factor continues to be the sound of the detonation of your own torpedoes."[25]

Deen Brown completed a total of eight war patrols on the *Trout*. The *Trout* was an effective hunter and was responsible for sinking over 37,000 tons of enemy shipping and twelve major vessels during her wartime career.[26] But an aggressive submarine also has more opportunities to experience depth charging, and Brown and the *Trout* experienced plenty of both. Radioman Brown became inured to the depth charge attacks and even a bit philosophical about them. Concerning depth charging, he related:

Initially, of course, I was scared like everybody else. But then I guess you get sort of battle hardened, we begin to learn how to gauge how close or how far from us they were. And after a while, you sort of just learn to accept it. And I didn't really have great fear of them anymore. But when they got real close and they started breaking light bulbs and glass on gages and things like that then that was a little worrisome. But then I woke up one morning and I thought, I'm merely being foolish. If I'm standing here, and I heard that blasted thing go off, I'm okay. It didn't kill me. I don't have to worry about it 'cause it's spent, and it's gone. The one I have to worry about is the one I haven't even heard. That's the next one. So I got along pretty good that way.[27]

Depth charges were still something to be feared, even once an accommodation had been made to them. But the most terrifying danger seems to have been attack from the air, either by enemy, or occasionally, by friendly aircraft. The beautifully clear water of the south Pacific allowed aircraft overhead to see submarines even when submerged. Brown reported that, "… those Japanese pilots, the fliers, could see us, say at down at one hundred feet depth. The water would be absolutely beautiful, it was so clear. But that didn't help us."[28] In fact, during a war patrol off of Truk Island, the *Trout* was severely damaged by an aerial attack that caused numerable non-repairable leaks, the loss of her navigational gyrocompasses, and rendered both periscopes inoperable. The boat had trouble performing a battery charge, typically done on the surface at night, because of the incessant harassment by enemy patrol craft. Only discovery of an enemy strategic flaw allowed them to complete a battery charge and retreat to the safety of the depths. Brown remembered, "For some reason or other those Japanese, especially those patrol boats which were something like one of our PC's [Patrol Craft] you know? They never looked aft in their wake. And so, when we discovered that, we would fall in a mile behind them or so in their wake and just follow them around. That way we could get in a battery charge."[29] The damaged Trout finally limped into Brisbane, Australia, escorted by another sub, the USS *Sailfish* (SS192), for rest and repairs.[30]

In addition to accumulating an impressive tonnage record and participating in the Doolittle Raid and Battle of Midway while Brown was onboard, the *Trout* made several runs to the Philippines to drop off Army Special Forces and ammunition to support the Filipino resistance efforts. Late in 1943, after completion of the *Trout's* tenth war patrol, Radioman Brown was ordered to report to Radar School to study the operation and maintenance of a new piece of equipment. The Radioman rating, at this time, was responsible for all of the electronic gear onboard, so Brown was assigned to master the intricacies of this piece of new technology. Brown left for radar school, and the USS *Trout* left for her eleventh war patrol. On April 17, 1944, the *Trout* was declared overdue and presumed lost.[31] Her precise fate remains unknown. Brown was accepting but obviously still troubled by the loss of his boat and his shipmates:

> ...they left me in to go to radar school, and they went on out, and I was supposed to return to the ship when they came back, but they didn't come back, so that's how I missed it. So I missed the *Nevada* because they sent me to radio school when it was bombed, and I missed the *Trout*, again because I was in school.[32]

Brown made one more patrol during the war on the USS *Gar* (SS 206). This brought his impressive total to nine war patrols. He was shipped out on the *Gar* because of a deal offered to him after the sink-

USS *Trout* underway, c. 1943.
Courtesy SFM

ing of the *Trout*. "The squadron personnel officer told me, 'Well, the *Gar* needs a senior Radioman, and you're the only one we've got.' He said, 'But if you'll make one patrol run on the *Gar*, when you get back in, I'll send you back to the States to commission a new boat under construction.' That sounded like a pretty good deal to me."[33] And a good deal it was, one made even better by the medical officer at the sub base in New London, Brown's new duty station. Radioman Brown, veteran of two years of constant front-line duty, was waiting for a reporting-in physical in a room full of new Submarine School recruits. This doctor looked at Brown, resplendent in full dress uniform complete with combat pin with nine stars, one for each war patrol, and medals and, of course the submarine qualification patch:

> "How many war patrols have you made?" I replied, "Well, Captain, I've made nine." The doctor said, "You made nine?" I said, "Yes, sir." So he gave me an examination, and he said, "You're not making any more." I looked at him, kind of stunned, you know? I said, "Well, does that mean there's something wrong with me?" He said, "You're too nervous."[34]

So thanks to this kindly and appreciative doctor, Brown's duties for the rest of the war were at the Submarine School, teaching the new submariners some of the skills he learned the hard way.

Brown remained in the navy after the war and enjoyed a series of, as he said, "real good assignments." Some of these included a tour of duty on the Admiral's staff and as the Submarine Squadron Ten Staff Chief Radioman. He married his wife, Lois, in 1947. He deliberately did not consider marriage during the war because, as he explained, "I wouldn't get married during the war. There were a lot of guys that would not. It was very plain that submarine business was a very risky business. One of the most risky businesses in the military. Our losses, you know, were the highest of any military unit. Almost twenty five percent of our people. So I had no inclination, whatsoever, to leave a widow. I wouldn't get married."[35]

When the war ended, Brown made the decision to stay in the navy, retiring after twenty-two years. In 1958, he was promoted to the newly created Master Chief rate; he was one of the first navy Chiefs and the only Radioman Chief in the Atlantic Submarine Force to achieve this new position. Brown maintained his connection with submarines by working at

Electric Boat shipyard in Groton, Connecticut, in the electrical engineering department for twenty-four years until retiring in 1987. Brown has maintained his connections with his shipmates and other submarine veterans as well, by his participation in the Submarine Veterans of World War II organization, in which he has held several leadership positions, including Connecticut State Commander. Brown concluded with the words, "I fought the war every night for years after the war was over." It was clear that the hardships and losses endured during the war were difficult to forget, and the pain they inflicted was slow to fade.

"Submarine guys had something real to do. Meaningful.
And that's what meant a lot to me; I wanted to do
something meaningful and real. Never mind the spit and polish."[36]

Deen Brown

DATE - 18 January 1943
SUBMARINE - USS TROUT
COMMANDING OFFICER - Lt Cdr L.P. RAMAGE, USN
SUBJECT: Prisoners taken from Japanese
            Schooner
POSITION - OFF INDO CHINA COAST

USS *Trout* crewmen topside with prisoners taken from
Japanese schooner, 18 January 1943.
Courtesy SFM

CHAPTER 8

"THE SELF-PROCLAIMED YOUNGSTER"

Warren Wildes (right) with his brother Russell Wildes, c. 1944.
Courtesy Warren Wildes

Name:	*Warren F. Wildes*
Born:	*1925*
Joined Navy:	*January, 1944*
Rating:	*Electrician's Mate*
Served On World War II	*USS* Flying Fish *(SS 229)*
Submarines:	*One War Patrol*
Service of Note:	*"Hell Cats" Invasion of the Sea of Japan, 1945*
Left Service:	*Discharged, 1946*

WARREN WILDES WAS the self-proclaimed "youngster" of his World War II submarine veteran peer group. At the young age of seventeen, he took advantage of a program by which young high school students with enough credits to graduate could leave school early and work in a defense plant. For Wildes, a native of the Noank section of Groton, Connecticut, that plant was Electric Boat, a primary designer and builder of submarines. A year later, he had enlisted in the navy, volunteered for submarines, and was headed for electrical training school at Purdue University. Wildes related about his motivation to be on subs, "I was attracted to submarines, you know, plus I knew that if I went to Sub School, I'd be close to home for a while. So I had a double motive, but I really did want, I did want submarines."[1]

After finishing his schooling in the top 10 percent of his class, Wildes became Electrician's Mate Third Class Wildes and was on his way to become a submarine relief crew member stationed at the Hunter's Point Naval Shipyard near San Francisco. Not content to simply be near the submarines, Warren attempted to get a billet onboard one of the fleet boats undergoing overhaul at the shipyard:

> I was desperate to get on the submarine, you know. The *Flying Fish* was in overhaul, and I was working on it as relief crew. I was helping a civilian electrician. So I walked up and asked somebody, "Could you use another Third Class Electrician?" They took me to the Chief, and the Chief took me to the Exec, and the next day, I was a member of the crew, and I tell you, I was walking on air. I tell you it was the thrill of a lifetime.[2]

Wildes's single war patrol was the twelfth for the USS *Flying Fish* (SS 229). Conducted between May and June of 1945, it was one of the most risky yet important multi-submarine missions of the war. The recently developed QLA or FM (frequency modulated) sonar was an extremely accurate but short-range underwater sound detection device. The submarines *Tinosa* and *Tunny* had previously demonstrated the effectiveness of the FM sonar in detecting mines. This new capability presented to the submarine fleet high command a new opportunity: the ability to successfully penetrate the minefields at the Tsushima Strait and enter the previously inviolate Sea of Japan.[3]

Wildes's boat, the *Flying Fish*, participated in this mission along with eight other submarines arranged in three groups. *Pierce's Pole Cats* consisted of the *Tunny*, *Skate*, and *Bonefish*, *Hydeman's Hep Cats* contained the submarines the *Sea Dog*, the *Crevalle*, and the *Spadefish,* and with the final group, commanded by the Captain of the *Flying Fish* went the *Bowfin* and the *Tinosa* and nicknamed *Risser's Bob Cats*.. Collectively, the nine-boat wolf pack was known as the *Hell Cats*. Their mission was to use their new sonar equipment to defeat the minefield at the Tsushima Strait, enter the Sea of Japan, split into the three groups, and proceed to their prearranged stations. At a prearranged time, they were to begin their attack on enemy shipping and hoped that the element of surprise would allow them to wreck havoc on the unsuspecting shipping.

In addition to the sonar, clearing wires were installed to "fair" the outline of the boats and remove projections that might cause mines to hang-up, be dragged, and ultimately explode. Some crewmen reported hearing the scrape of the mine wine as it dragged along the clearing wires; hearing the slow scraping of chain on wire and agonizingly waiting for the explosion. Wildes reported, "It was scary. A couple of boats actually felt the scraping, you know," but he qualified his answer, "I don't think we did. One or two guys claimed they did. I don't know if they really did."[4] This passage through the Tsushima Strait was, by far, the most stressful part of the entire mission. Warren Wildes in the *Flying Fish* entered the minefield in the last group and completed the transit in about sixteen hours.

One of Wildes's shipmates was the Radioman in charge of operating the FM sonar during the passage. According to Wildes, "He was an expert sound man, and he got the Bronze Star. He was the only enlisted man to ever get a medal on the *Flying Fish* in the whole history of *Flying Fish*."[5] The sonar operator was essential to the operation in maintaining the sensitive equipment operating and translating the information produced by the sonar into mine-avoiding course changes. Then the helmsman would make these minute changes in course and plot a path of safety through the deadly field. The helmsman on the *Flying Fish* during this dangerous maneuver was a diminutive character named Holloway, nicknamed "Half-Hitch." Wildes remembers that at the end of the minefield transit, the Captain got on the intercom and announced to the ship, "We're through the minefields; Half-Hitch brought us through." He also recalled how Half-Hitch got his nickname:

I gave it to him. During World War II there was a little one-panel cartoon in *Navy Times* about a little sailor four feet tall called Half-Hitch. Had hair across his forehead, a cowlick, and he looked just like him. When I saw him, I nicknamed him that and, in fact, it stuck with him until he died. His wife called him Hitch, yeah, that was his nickname. He was a wonderful friend. I sure miss him.[6]

Once into the Sea of Japan, the boats headed for their attack stations. The *Hep Cats* patrolled the western coast of Hokkaido and Honshu, the *Pole Cats* went to southern and central Honshu, and the *Bob Cats*, with Warren and the *Flying Fish*, were sent to the east coast of Korea.[7] During this mission, the combined *Hell Cat* pack sank a total of twenty-eight ships; more than 54,000 tons of enemy shipping. This was one of the most successful submarine operations of the entire war, due in part to the lack of anti-submarine preparation within the sea. The Japanese military considered the Sea of Japan impenetrable and "Hirohito's private bathtub,"[8] as this body of water was called by the men, had not been violated by Allied warships since September of 1943, when the legendary *Wahoo*, commanded by Dudley "Mush" Morton, was sunk trying to exit the sea through the northern La Perouse Strait[9]. Wildes confirmed, "We were inside the inland Sea of Japan where no other boat had even been except the *Wahoo* .... But you know their ships [Japanese] had their running lights on. They never dreamed anybody would ever get in there."[10]

After one successful torpedo attack on June 11, 1945, resulted in the sinking of the Japanese cargo ship *Meisei Maru*, the *Flying Fish* recovered a single Japanese soldier from the water. The Captain wrote in his war patrol report, "Took aboard one superior private of the Japanese Army. He was the only one of about twenty-four survivors who responded to repeated calls of, 'Don't be afraid, climb aboard' in the C.O.'s best Japanese."[11] As was typical, most of these Japanese survivors of a sinking would rather drown than be taken prisoner, due to their fear of torture, and dread of loss of honor. This man was no exception as Wildes recalled of his rescue:

It took us three hours just to get him to agree to come out of the water, and the water was very cold. One of the officers said that there was a couple of hundred [Japanese sailors] in the water, whether how many were soldiers and how many were crew members [I don't know]. We hit them around midnight, so this guy [the Japanese prisoner] was practically naked when we brought him down through the hatch. He was — gosh, he was only about this tall, he was scared to death, I'm telling you, because he thought, if you read that letter, you see that he expected to be tortured. And he figured that he had disgraced himself...[12]

Communication with the prisoner was mostly through gestures and displaying numbers. As the Captain noted, "He can say 'Thank you, sir' but professes no knowledge of English or Romaji [the use of the Latin alphabet to write the Japanese language]. Makes hen tracks beautifully and uses Arabic numerals — the latter a big help."[13] After medical care, rest, and other humane considerations, the prisoner was set to work polishing the torpedo tubes. This was an exercise in "busy work" as the torpedo tubes, except for the hatch, were never polished, though their bronze construction did allow them to achieve a dazzling shine with the appropriate application of effort. This kept the prisoner busy and allowed the Forward Torpedo Room to win a contrived "shiny tube" contest with the After Torpedo Room.[14] However, even though the work had no military value, Wildes remembered that it caused the Japanese man distress. "He didn't like polishing those [torpedo] tubes. He thought that was aiding the war effort. They would have worked with or without [the polishing].[15]

A letter written by the Japanese soldier himself while he was onboard confirmed Wildes's opinion. The prisoner stated that he found the work on the submarine's military equipment, "distressing," but it also showed his real affection for the crew and his appreciation of their kindness and friendship:

The force that made me feel this strong friendship seemed to be the unlimited humanity of your crew. It is the enormous capacity for friendship that these men have. As the days passed the intensity of this feeling grew, and in less than a month I was led to the point where I cried many times from gratitude. If there had been no language barrier, I would have been eloquent in my words of gratitude.[16]

And the feeling was mutual. Warren Wildes remembered, "... I think it's very, very profound what he says. The message he's giving us. Thanking us profusely for treating him humanely, and how he hoped that this war would end all wars, and so forth and so on. Nice little guy."[17]

Although the crew of the *Flying Fish* was dedicated to the destruction of the Japanese war capability and the preservation of American security, they did not exhibit any apparent hate toward the Japanese individual, even as a soldier of the Japanese military. Wildes displayed this in his positive and complementary comments. Also, in his description of this event on the *Flying Fish*, author and crewmate Dale Russell commented on the humane and encouraging treatment the crew gave to their prisoner. For instance, the time when he refused to eat, "The prisoner refused to partake of some soup, until (crewman) Evans took a swallow, then he readily accepted the soup."[18]

The crew of the *Flying Fish* had captured their prisoner after a successful attack on a Japanese cargo ship. But not all of their attacks were successful, and some of them involved a large amount of risk and expenditure of torpedoes, all for no gain. One of these frustrating attacks occurred on June 20, 1945, in the harbor of Seishin, now called Chongjin, with the result of an undamaged target, torpedoes detonating harmlessly on the beach, and an extended pursuit by angered harbor defenders. According to Wildes:

> The worst experience we had, we went into a harbor, very shallow water, maybe twelve fathoms, and there was a tanker tied up at the dock, you know, good sized tanker. We fired two fish at it. They went right underneath it and hit the beach. We heard them hit the beach and explode. So we turned around, and a patrol boat got on us and chased us out of there. But we got out. He didn't get close to us. He dropped a few charges, but there was never a — never any danger. A lot of guys experienced a hell of a lot worse than that.[19]

This failure aside, she had sunk two large enemy freighters, and when these larger targets were not to be found, the men of the *Flying Fish* turned their attention to the smaller coastal shipping, not as glamorous, but an important conduit of supplies to the Japanese home islands. For these battle-surface actions, Warren was assigned duties to prepare the boat to surface:

> And then when we surfaced, my battle station was in the pump room, and I went down there, and when we hit the surface I had to turn on the low pressure air compressor to take the pressure off the boat. You know, because the pressure builds up, and if you open that hatch it would send you flying out through. Just to relieve the pressure, I started it up, maybe two or three minutes, and then they'd open the hatch. And then I was the backup ammunition loader in the after battery. It went up through the hull. It was stored below the galley, we had shells stored down below the galley.[20]

Most of these smaller enemy cargo vessels were too small to justify expenditure of a expensive torpedo, so the deck guns were used to sink them, most often after the enemy crew had been warned to abandon their ship. The *Flying Fish* made effective use of these surface operations, as Warren remembered, "And then we sunk about twelve small craft with our deck gun. Sampans, barges. Our orders were anything that was possibly of benefit to the enemy, to sink it."[21]

The *Flying Fish* and the rest of the subs of the *Hell Cats*, their assignment complete, moved to rendezvous at the entrance to the La Perouse Strait. This northern egress from the Sea of Japan divides the southern part of the Russian island of Sakhalin from the northern part of the Japanese island of Hokkaido. The strait is about twenty-five miles long and from sixty to one hundred and twenty feet deep; too shallow for a submerged transit. The pack members formed up, ready to make the risky transit, but one submarine was not there. The *Bonefish*, part of the *Pole Cat* group, failed to appear at the appointed time. Wildes recalled waiting for the missing sub, with some emotion, "...the *Bonefish* was the only one that didn't show up. And the *Tunny*, one of the boats that was in the operation, the *Tunny* stayed around and went back in to try to make radio contact, but never did. So they're still there. Anyway... I get emotional every time I talk about it."[22] The *Tunny's* war patrol report was terse when describing this poignant event:

25 June 1945:	(continued)
2030	Sent message to *BONEFISH*.
2130	Sent message to *BONEFISH* again.[23]

Eventually, even the faithful *Tunny* had to accept that her pack-mate was not coming home. It is believed that after successfully sinking her first ship of the mission, the *Bonefish* entered Toyama Bay, a shallow body of water. There she sank another large ship, but in doing so alerted the Japanese anti-submarine forces, whose vicious depth charge retaliation probably finally sank the *Bonefish*.[24] Part of the enduring pain for those who had shipmates or loved ones lost on one of the fifty-two submarines sunk during World War II was the lack of absolute confirmation of their sinking. Certainly, when a boat like the *Bonefish* failed to show up for a scheduled rendezvous and failed to report to her home base, it was a near certainty that they had run afoul of an enemy ship or plane. However, instead of receiving confirmation that a son or husband's ship had sunk, the only report that was given to the home front was that a sub was "Overdue and Presumed Lost."[25]

The *Hell Cats* pack, smaller by one, made their escape through the shallow La Perouse Strait at night and on the surface. This tense and dangerous passage was made at full speed, in a dense fog, and without incident. At the same time as the transit was occurring, Admiral Lockwood, the submarine force commander, had the sub USS *Trutta* shell the island of *Hirado Shima* near the mission's entrance at the *Tsushima* Strait in a "purposely conspicuous manner." This diversion may have led the Japanese to believe that the *Hell Cats* were leaving through the same door that they entered.[26] The uneventful end to the mission within the Sea of Japan was more stressful for Wildes than the beginning had been. "To me, that was a scarier exit, exiting was scarier than going in because of the noise, you know, the four main engines running at flank speed."[27]

The *Flying Fish* and the remainder of the *Hell Cats*, except the *Tunny*, ended this war patrol in Midway on June 30, 1945. The *Tunny* had been given permission to remain in the Sea of Okhotsk for an additional two days to wait for, and call for, the *Bonefish*. When these efforts proved fruitless, the *Tunny* joined the rest of the *Hell Cats* on July 2. The remaining pack proceeded to Pearl Harbor to receive the praise and gratitude of the Pacific Submarine Commander.

USS *Flying Fish* (SS 229) after twelfth war patrol flying battle flag,
c. July 1945.
Courtesy SFM

After a brief rest period, Wildes was headed back to the Sea of Japan
on the *Flying Fish*, but not with the same enthusiasm that existed for
the first trip. "I don't the think the second time that we were going to
be in there [the Sea of Japan] they were going to be very receptive."

Fortunately for Wildes and the *Flying Fish*, they never had to
find out just how receptive the Japanese would be. While making the
transit, the atomic bombs were dropped on Hiroshima and Nagasaki,
forcing the Imperial Japanese capitulation and ending the war. Wildes
was matter-of-fact about his feelings toward this new weapon.
"When the war ended, we were heading back to the Sea of Japan, and
we were about half way to Guam. We get this telegram from Forre-
stal, who was the Secretary of War, saying the war was over. They
turned us around, and we went back to Pearl Harbor. So I figure that
bomb saved my life, I'll tell you that."[28]

Wildes's single war patrol was full of excitement and adventure, but there was still plenty of time for the more mundane, but important aspects of life, like food. Aboard the *Flying Fish*, "Food was pretty good, it wasn't as great as everyone makes it out to be." according to Wildes. "I think it depended on who was doing it. We had a Baker that was terrific, a First Class [petty officer] Baker. And we used to look forward to his stuff, but we had a couple of Cooks that were not the greatest." Wildes acknowledged, though, that the Cooks often didn't have that much space or material to work with. "It was tough, it was tough to, you know, the galley, for God's sake was about as big as right here. Awfully tight quarters. Well, we didn't starve to death; there was no problem that way."[29] Also, as was typical, hygiene during a war patrol ranged from unique to nonexistent. Enlisted men would sometime bathe using a bucket of always precious water if available. Mostly, they became inured to the conditions onboard which would have been unendurable if they had not developed gradually. Warren's shipmate, Dale Russell, wrote of this condition:

After reaching the hotel [after a war patrol], I realized that I had left my wristwatch on my bunk [onboard]. I had been on shore long enough to clear my nostrils of all the boat's disagreeable odors and was met by a very obvious and disagreeable stench at the hatch entrance. With limited fresh air circulating, the accumulation of various odors trapped in the relatively small interior grew into a massive stench. However, the odor coming from the interior of the *Flying Fish* was difficult to accept.[30]

Fleet submarines were designed and built with showers, but the lack of plentiful fresh water rendered them useless except for storage space. Wildes commented, "Well, we had showers, but they were full of potatoes, nobody took a shower when we were out to sea I'll tell you that. We needed it, but we didn't."[31]

Mail was always an important aspect of this ship's morale, and Wildes remembers that its prompt delivery always seemed to be a priority. "Yeah, every time we got to a port, you know, like Midway, when we got to Midway I got a bunch of mail from my parents, built up you know. And my girlfriend, who later dumped me, but, it came through pretty good."[32]

Wildes, as an Electrician's Mate on a fleet submarine, had many duties related to the electrical systems and equipment onboard. The maintenance of the storage batteries, necessary for extended submerged operations, also consumed most of the available fresh water and was a typical and constant duty for an Electrician. Work on the batteries also made the Electricians easy to identify from the rest of the crew, since the acid would eat holes in whatever uniform they were wearing. Another duty was to stand watch as Auxiliary Electrician. Wildes related one story that illuminated one of the details of his duties and explained the source of at least one of the many unusual submarine odors. It also showed the ability of submariners to find humor even in the most regrettable situations:

> One of the duties of the Auxiliary Electrician is to blow the sanitary tank during the — you know, when everybody was asleep, during the night. So I went in, went through the routine of closing the flappers and closing the doors. Well, right in the middle of it, our Quartermaster got called to the bridge. He came rolling out of his bunk, he come [*sic*] back, and he walked in [to the head] and opened that flapper, and, I'm telling you, it just blew all over him. That poor guy, I tell you, I felt so sorry for him. He came stumbling into the crew's mess, and he had a beard, and it was dripping. He didn't say a word to me, he just washed himself off, cleaned himself up, and took off. But that happened — once in a while that happened. But I happened to be the operator that time. I felt bad. But if you had to blow it submerged, you had to vent it inboard, and I tell you that absolutely woke everybody up, the smell was awful, as we always tried to do it while we were on the surface. Planned it that way, if we could. But I'll never forget that night. Joe Lort his name was. Ugh. Wow. That woke him up, that's for sure.[33]

The war over, the *Flying Fish* was sent back to the States and became a school boat for the Submarine School in New London, Connecticut. Warren served on her in this capacity until the USS *Corporal* (SS 346), which had just gone into commission, needed an Electrician to assist them for a shake-down cruise. Petty Officer Wildes was transferred, and the next day was headed for Panama.

He spent about six months of this "good duty" on the *Corporal* before being discharged from the navy, and apparently, was not in a terrible rush to get out. "I was, what'd they say, 'duration and six', that's what they used to say, duration of the war plus six. Yeah, I was in longer than that, but anyway, I enjoyed that. We went down to Key West, Panama, Guantanamo, it was like a pleasure cruise. We'd play softball..."[34]

Wildes met his wife of more than sixty years under very unique circumstances after he left the navy. He went out to California with a buddy from Groton to visit two other Groton boys whose families had relocated there during the war. While these four boys were there, they met four girls, nurses, from New London, Connecticut, who were also vacationing in California. One of these girls was Wildes's future wife. The fact that these two Connecticut exports met each other three thousand miles away from home, fell in love, and got married is a curious enough story. But the amazing part of this romantic tale is that all four of those Groton boys married all four of those New London girls. Wildes related, "Well, not only me, but there were three other boys, and they all married these. My wife was a graduate nurse from Lawrence Hospital, and they went out as a group, four of them, and we married them all. Wasn't that something? I told my wife, 'You were out there swimming back and forth like sharks waiting for us to get there.' "[35]

Wildes and his wife continue to live in Groton, nearly in the shadow of Electric Boat shipyard where he began his affair with submarines. He loved his career on submarines, but is keenly aware of the closing of that chapter in our nation's history as the submarine veterans pass away or, as the veteran's organization phrases it, depart on eternal patrol.

"I was attracted to submarines, you know, plus I knew that if I went to Sub School I'd be close to home for a while. So I had a double motive but I really did want, I did want submarines."[36]

Warren Wildes

Photo taken aboard USS *Flying Fish* (SS 229) in maneuvering room during 12th war patrol in WW II, location inland Sea of Japan, June, 1945. Left to right, Nelvin Lusse EM 2/c, George "Kinko" Sunbury RM 1/c, Warren F. Wildes EM 3/c.
Courtesy Warren Wildes

CHAPTER 9

"THE ABSENT COMPANION"

Harry F. Julian, in dress blues, home in Deep River, CT,
c. February, 1944.
Courtesy SFM

Name:	*Harry F. Julian*
Born:	*1926*
Joined Navy:	*January, 1944*
Rating:	*Torpedoman's Mate*
Served On World War II	*USS* Snook *(SS 279)*
Submarines:	*Three War Patrols*
Overdue and Presumed Lost:	*April 8, 1945*

119

HARRY JULIAN WAS the absent companion. A Torpedoman's Mate onboard the USS *Snook* (SS 279), Harry and his boat were declared overdue and presumed lost on her ninth war patrol. What is known of Harry comes from a collection of over one hundred of his letters to his mother and father, lovingly preserved, and now residing in the U.S. Navy Submarine Force Museum. The conversation is poignantly one-sided, since all of the letters to Harry remained with him onboard *Snook*. He was an attentive correspondent, devoted to his family and girlfriend, and, apparently, always hungry. He is a typical American sailor of the time; eager for fun, proud of his boat, and missing his home. While he follows scrupulously the censor regulations of wartime, one can glimpse inside his world, through these letters, and understand better the more mundane aspects of World War II submarine duty.

Harry's first letter was written on June 25, 1943, at 3 PM in New Haven, Connecticut, on the train to the U.S. Naval Training Station at Camp Sampson, New York, bound for recruit training. He wrote primarily to his mother in his hometown of Deep River, Connecticut. At Camp Sampson, he was processed in and underwent the typical boot camp training designed to quickly convert the undisciplined civilian into a competent military man. As was also typical, he was both disturbed and pleased by certain aspects of his changed appearance. He wrote of his haircut, "My new haircut is absolutely the nuts. To show you how unique it is. When someone asks me where I'm from I say 'I'm from hunger,' and they believe me." But of his new clothing he says, "My uniforms fit good and I look pretty good in them if I say so myself."[1]

Harry had a good sense of humor and often related amusing things that happened around him, in addition to his chronicle of regular navy events. He wrote to his sister about going to see the movies while at Sampson:

> The movies here are very different than civilian movies. We yell and holler and whistle and everything. They don't cost anything and we go twice a week. Last night I saw Deanna Durbin in her latest and in one place she appears clad in a thin nighty. You should here [sic] the boys yell. And every time a sailor comes on the screen the place roars.[2]

As was usual with all recruits, much of Harry's boot camp day was consumed by drilling, cleaning, inspections, and the necessary medical examinations and inoculations. Additionally, various intelligence and aptitude tests were administered to determine if the recruits were suited for specialized training. Harry had several ratings he was interested in, but he eventually chose Torpedoman's Mate and, on August 29, he found out that he was selected for this training. "I have finally been drafted for Torpedoman School. Yesterday we went to get a physical for it." He continued, "When we got to the dispensary we were informed that those of us that passed the physical they were about to give us would be sent not only to torpedo but also Submarine School. We had no choice on the matter. Those who qualified were simply being drafted. The reason, no doubt, is because that can't get enough volunteers."[3]

Since all submarine sailors must be volunteers, two explanations may be surmised from Harry's characterization of his being "drafted" into submarines. The first is that since he selected the Torpedoman rating, he may have been required to volunteer if he wanted this rating and the accompanying schooling. To request Torpedoman but refuse to volunteer for subs may have been too restrictive a condition for the navy based on the wartime condition and the needs of the service. Second, he may have been disavowing his direct involvement to diffuse the anger his mother must have felt at him for volunteering for such a dangerous naval occupation. There is some evidence for this in Harry's statement in the same letter, "Please don't worry about this because subs aren't as bad as you think they are. There have been very few subs sunk in the war. You were willing to have me try to be a pilot and pilots live lot shorter lives than sub men. Beside it's an honor to be a sub man."[4]

Harry's other experiences in recruit training are typical to the regimented atmosphere, with the exception of his humorously keen interest in food, his ongoing quest for the alleviation of hunger, and his eagerness for the receipt of comfort packages from home as evidenced in his letters:

We had pie twice today. Don't know what's going to happen

For chow today we had some kind of very dead fish that was not extremely tasty. Since I didn't take much I went down to ships service afterward and had 6 doughnuts and a pint of chocolate milk. Price 25¢. They have a doughnut machine and it really makes tasty doughnuts

Can't think of much else to write except one request. ~~Please send me~~ [sic] something to eat. Just buy a lot of stuff and put it in a box.

I have been awfully busy the whole week or I would have written you. Since our company is mess cook company we really work. And hard!! I worked 18 hours yesterday and still had pep after I got through. Maybe because I had about two cherry pies and quarts of milk to drink. We get all we can eat.

Do not worry about my not getting enough to eat because I do. Only sometimes, due to my new found enormous appetite, I am not completely satisfied. The food you give up does come to us. Should I say more?

You seem to be filled with righteous indignation over the food I am not supposed to be getting. I am sorry I misinformed you. Don't start hating the gov. because we do get the best food obtainable.

I didn't get that package, you said you were going to send, yet. Maybe those dumb mail clerks helped themselves to it. I wouldn't trust them.[5]

Harry's dissatisfaction, apparently, was only directed at the enemies of his stomach, as was clear when he wrote, "There isn't anything I don't like, though. The Navy takes darn good care of you."[6]

On September 5, 1943, Harry Julian arrived in the Norfolk Operational Base in Norfolk, Virginia, to begin Torpedoman Training School. Typical for Harry, in his first letter he assessed the quality of the Norfolk culinary services as he wrote, "The chow here is wonderful. Compared to Sampson chow this is like the food of the gods.[7] The school was ten weeks long and consisted generally in learning the design, operation, and maintenance of the torpedo. Both surface and submarine bound sailors attended this school without distinction, as the weapon was the same for both applications. Only the last two weeks, torpedo aiming, were waived for those destined for submarines as the tubes were not individually aimed; the entire vessel was moved into an appropriate firing position.

Since this Fleet Service School was considered advanced training, those who failed two progress exams were dropped from the course and sent to the fleet for general assignment. Passing the course, especially with high marks, meant immediate and more rapid promotions and more desirable duty assignments. Harry was aware of the benefits of doing well in the school and expressed some early apprehension at the task in front of him. He wrote, "A torpedo is a comparatively small thing but complicated! Holy cripes! What a mess. We are having a test Saturday morning. I hope I pass. I guess I will."[8]

While Harry was at Norfolk, an accidental explosion occurred at the Naval Air Station nearby, on September 17, 1943. An overloaded ordnance department truck was pulling four trailers of depth charges on the air station's taxiway. One of the explosives came loose, fell, and was dragged against the road. Despite attempts to cool the depth charges, they began exploding, killing some firefighters who were attempting to extinguish the burning devices. The depth charges exploded for several minutes, and the concussion from the blast broke windows seven miles away. Harry, not directly involved in this incident, related his perceptions to his mother:

> You have probably heard about the blast that wreck [*sic*] the air field here. The airfield is about a mile and a half from us so we really heard it. It was caused by exploding depth charges and was quite a bang. 25 people are dead from it one of them a Wave. Friday morning we were sitting in school and all of a sudden bulooey!! [*sic*] The walls of the school even gave in with the concussion. One C.P.O. who had been in most of the major battles (I overheard this) hit the dirt and laid on his face just from instinct or something.[9]

Seaman Second Class Harry Julian did well in Torpedoman School maintaining above a 3.0 average throughout the course. He related in his letters an appropriate amount of grousing, tension, and fear of doing well and mastering the complicated technology of the torpedo. His fears were misplaced, as he discovered on November 13, 1943, as he graduated from Torpedoman School, with a grade of 3.41 on his final exam, and was promoted to Seaman First Class (S 1/c). After graduation, he was assigned to report to Submarine School in New London, Connecticut. He completed Sub School successfully, but provided no written details of this experience. A native of Deep River, a mere eighteen miles from New London, his communications with family, friends, and his sweetheart Joan, could be and were face-to-face. If his experience was typical, Harry learned the basics of submarine operation, including the general design and layout of the boats, duties onboard, and basic operations of the submarine. Near the end of the course, Harry would have been taken out into Long Island Sound on older "school boats" and given practice in common procedures like surface running, diving the boat, and operating submerged. This general orientation allowed the students to gain the minimum knowledge required before beginning the real learning once onboard an operating submarine.

Harry traveled in a troop sleeper train across country to Mare Island Shipyard in California, approximately thirty miles northeast of San Francisco. As was often the case, he became a member of one of the submarine relief crews in Submarine Division Eighty One. Now an official, though unqualified, submariner, he began to draw extra submarine pay and continued sending money home and buying war bonds. It was clear that this Connecticut boy was immediately smitten by the many attractions of sunny California and the large Mare Island base when he writes, "The food is wonderful here and everything is so convenient and easy to get at that it is practically a Utopia or somethin' [*sic*]."[10]

As a member of a relief crew, Harry would relieve the regular crew of a sub just back from a war patrol from their watch and maintenance duties. His first assignment was on the USS *Seal* (SS 183), and he wrote, "I am in the relief crew of the U.S.S. *Seal* which has been out for a long time and at present is tied up alongside the dock getting a complete overhaul. She is an older boat and will become a school boat for New London, I think. I stand watches on her and work there in the day time."[11] Harry described types of shipboard work that would be familiar to any sailor; chipping paint, moving equipment, and standing guard duty. These mundane tasks detracted in no way from his enthusiasm for being a member of the submarine force, which he made clear when he wrote home, "I am as well as ever and am feeling over virile in my new role as son of the sea and submarine man extraordinary. Ha ha. It must be glandular or something.[12]

His work on the *Seal* was a temporary assignment, and though members of relief crews very often lobbied commanders of boats in from patrol for a permanent berth, Harry was not to become a member of this submarine's crew. His letters about the *Seal* raised hopes at home, though, of the possibility of him returning to New London, since Harry had mentioned that the *Seal* might be heading there to become a school boat for the Submarine School. He disabused them of this notion when he wrote, "Someone back there has a mistaken idea that I might be assigned to the *Seal* and that any day now I'll be coming back to Conn. Don't let me deflate your dream bubbles or something but I won't get assigned to the *Seal* and I won't be coming back to Conn. for a long, long time. I am headed out of the states some day but I don't know when."[13]

As is clear by the volume and frequency of his correspondence, mail was a huge morale booster for Harry. Throughout his letters, he expressed his thanks to the writers, mostly his mother, for the frequent letters. He would also be irritable when he got none, even when he seemed to know that delay in mail delivery was caused by something he had done, whether it was a change of duty station, extended sea time, or other circumstance. After settling in at Mare Island, he commented, "I've been getting Joanie's letters in two days also. That's pretty fast. We get mail pretty nice here. You can get it anytime even on Sunday. That is if you've got any. And I usually have some.[14]

On May 19, 1944, and without explanation on how this was accomplished, Harry writes as a member of the crew of the USS *Snook* (SS 279). "As you can see I am now a member of the crew of the *Snook*. I am getting pretty salty."[15] The *Snook* was a *Gato* class submarine that had been commissioned in October of 1942. When Harry joined the boat, she had just completed her fifth war patrol and was sent to the San Francisco Naval Shipyard, at Hunter's Point in San Francisco, for a major overhaul. The *Snook* was a skilled hunter, sinking seventeen major enemy vessels and amassing over 75,000 tons of destroyed shipping during her eight war patrols.[16] During this major overhaul, the *Snook* received a thorough repair and restoration

Harry F. Julian and Joan "Joanie" P. Nelson in Deep River,
CT, c. February, 1944.
Courtesy SFM

of her battle-worn equipment and some structural repair work was
certainly done to the bow of the sub to repair the impact damage
caused when Captain C.O. Triebel struck the pier while mooring. A
rare glimpse into confidential submarine activity was revealed when
Seaman Julian bypassed the naval censor by mailing his letter in a
civilian mailbox. His information was relatively benign and without
strategic significance, but he showed an uncharacteristic lapse of discipline when he wrote, "I'm not living on board the boat yet because
it's in dry dock as a result of the skipper ramming the dock. I couldn't
say much in last night's letter because I mailed it through the censor."
A letter to his sister Barbara also bypassed the censor and related
more details about his attitude toward this new assignment on the
Snook:

Popular opinion is that it is a lousy boat but I'm optomistic [*sic*] and think it's alright. We went out for trials in the bay Wed. Everything went okay except that when we were coming along side the dock the skipper didn't back down on the engines fast enough so we rammed the dock. Made a hell of a hole in the dock but just bent up the bow a little. That is why it's in dry dock now.[17]

The practice of avoiding the censor appears to have been typical though, as Harry continues in the letter to his parents, "This censoring is a lot of hogwash but it's just the navy way I guess. We do mail them on the beach when we get a chance." [18]

Harry was obviously excited as he helped prepare the *Snook* for her sixth war patrol. He wrote, "I'm sitting in the crew's mess writing this. We moved aboard this morning and now I'm really on a ship. We have all our stores aboard and the ship is all fueled and ready for sea. Tonight I've got the duty but tomorrow night I haven't and since it is my last night I think I'll go [on] a spree and buy myself a lot of necessary gear." His eagerness is evident as he comments about another submarine, recently returned from sea. "The USS *Trigger* pulled in today with 36 Jap flags flying and shark mouth painted on her bow. Also a Brassier [brassiere] tied to her periscope. The navy always comes through. I hope we can do as well."[19]

Before the excitement of the war patrol, Harry had to concern himself with the more mundane duties of the new crew member. To guide, direct, and occasionally force him to learn the ways of the sub was his "Sea Daddy." This was typically a more senior member of the same department or rating who was assigned responsibility for a new crew member, especially one who had never before gone to sea. The Sea Daddy could be paternalistic, as the name implies, or he could be a tyrant. Harry appeared to be lucky enough to have had one of the former in the person of Torpedoman First Class Keith Allen Bjerk. "My Sea Daddy "Pinky" Bjerk of North Dakota told me to tell you hello so hello for Pinky. He's a big 1st class Torpedoman and is a pretty good guy. He is also the ship's barber. He cut my hair short the other night and did a good job." And every new submariner had to take his turn in the galley; mess cooking it is called. Part prep-chef, part scullery maid and general server, cleaner and laborer for all of the nasty and necessary jobs the sub's kitchen requires, the mess cooking duties were as much a rite of passage as they were a necessary first job onboard. Harry summed it up for his mom, "My mess cooking duties are still keeping me busy from dawn till dusk. And I used to hate washing dishes – Man Oh man!" But, as was always important to Harry, on the *Snook* the food was good and plentiful, and he expresses his contentment succinctly, "I'm eating more than I ever ate before and living like a king. A slightly cramped king that is."[20]

The *Snook* left for her sixth war patrol on June 25, 1944, and was assigned to patrol the areas south of Honshu and Shikoku and also the approaches to *Kii Suido* and *Bungo Suido*, straits on the west and east ends of the island of Shikoku.[21] Harry bid farewell to "Mom & Pop" with the following reassurance. "Well, we're getting ready to go again so you probably won't be getting any letters from me for a long long time. Don't worry about me because I'll be okay."[22] This war patrol was a disappointing one for the usually productive *Snook*. Two attacks produced no sinkings, and a lack of targets caused the *Snook* to return home empty-handed. The patrol was classified "unsuccessful," the first time she failed to sink any enemy shipping since her commissioning.

Crew & Battle Flag - USS *Snook* c. 1944.
Harry, center-left, with mark on hat.
Courtesy SFM

However, Harry seemed to have enjoyed his first submarine voyage. He wrote, "Well, here is your long lost son and heir again still able to write, as you can see. I've been at sea and unable to write.... I'm okay all around with no complaints whatsoever." He didn't dwell on the moments of terror during his first war experience but suggested in his writing that he might have had some close calls. "I can see now why they pay 50% more for sub service. It isn't too bad but its awful tiring at times. The Julian in me predominated a couple of times and I was quite frightened but I got over it."[23]

On September 1, 1944, the *Snook* left on her seventh war patrol. Harry informed his parents, "Well here is the last letter you'll get for a long time. It will be about sixty days or more."[24] He actually was able to send two more letters during this patrol; one around September 14, possibly from Saipan, and one on September 24, again probably from Saipan where the *Snook* stopped for repairs until October 4.[25] His communications were by necessity cryptic, as when he wrote, "Well I got another chance to write so here goes. Have been to some strange places I can't disclose but have been headlines of late."[26] During this war patrol, the *Snook* sank three major enemy ships; the passenger-cargo ship *Shinsei Maru Number 1*, the tanker *Kikusui Maru*, and the cargo ship *Arisan Maru*. Though the crew of the *Snook* was unaware of this at the time of the attack, the *Arisan Maru* was a "hell ship" transporting American prisoners of war from areas previously held by the Japanese. These hell ships were notorious for the conditions onboard that caused incredible loss of life due to asphyxia, starvation, or dysentery. These ships carried no markings to identify them as prisoner transports. The sinking of the *Arisan Maru* caused the loss of life of over 1,800 American P.O.W.s, making it one of the greatest losses of life in American maritime history.[27]

Harry returned to his correspondence at the end of the *Snook's* seventh war patrol on November 14, 1944. Respectful of the rules of censorship, he summed up his experiences with the following terse paragraph:

> Well the usuall [*sic*] things have been happening to me. None of which I can write here. I can say I've made another patrol. I also can say that we rescued a flier, but that's all. You'll have to use your imaginations to make the story complete.[28]

In this letter, he also let his parents know that he had qualified in submarines. That achievement allowed Harry to wear the embroidered dolphins on his right sleeve, midway between the wrist and elbow, the visible mark of the qualified submariner. In addition, the completion of a successful war patrol allowed him to wear a silver submarine combat patrol pin over his ribbons above the left breast pocket of his uniform. Though fairly ubiquitous in today's navy, these special insignia were extremely rare among enlisted men in the World War II era and helped set the submariner apart as a member of an elite organization.

TM 3/c Harry Julian on liberty in Hawaii wearing white jumper with Torpedoman Third Class rating badge, submarine qualification "Dolphin" patch, and war patrol pin, c. 1944.
Courtesy SFM

Harry was usually more concerned about more commonplace matters. In one letter, he reported that the civilian underwear he received, a fulfilled request from an earlier letter, continued to provide him good service and, apparently, some amusement for his crewmates in the Forward Torpedo Room. He wrote, "The jock shorts are holding out exceptionally well. I've got my name stenciled all over them to make sure they don't get lost by intention in some of the laundries we patronize. The guys up here that wear those regulation misfits call them my sexy skivvies."[29] Harry had also signed up for correspondence courses so that he could finish high school during the war. He started with English Literature and several other courses, but found it difficult to work on the assignments at sea. "The high school will have to wait I guess. I can't do anything out here." Harry complained.[30]

Although serious business was the usual order of the day in their engineering surroundings, the boys in the Forward Torpedo Room of the *Snook* still looked forward to Christmas. Harry mentioned that they planned on "manufacturing" a replica tree if they could not acquire something better. Mom and Dad came through and actually sent Harry what sounds like a small cedar tree, which elicited joy from the recipient and his mates. "The cedar tree was very dry but still smelled cedarish and Connecticutish [*sic*]. Jack Reagan [*sic*][31] agreed that it smelled just like home." Harry wrote, and "Regan and I smelled it like two Ferdinands and dreamed of oak clad hills etc."[32] On December 16, 1944, Harry informed his parents that the navy gave him an early Christmas present in the form of a promotion to Torpedoman's Mate, Third Class (TM 3/c). "Mr. McNiel Macniel[33] something like that anyhow who was assistant gunnery officer told me the other day that I did make 3/c so I guess I'm a TM now.[34] This rank, equivalent to that of an army corporal, was the entry level of the Petty Officer ranks. As a Third Class Petty Officer, Harry was, by this promotion, confirmed in his rating and expected to assume more responsibility, especially for other subordinate members of the weapons department. In addition to the promotion, Harry enumerated the other presents he received in a letter home dated December 23, 1944:

Santa Claus sent 9 packages in all, so far to me for which I was very, very grateful. The books both arrived but have not been read yet. Saving them for next run. The fudge spoiled (covered with mildew) and punuchi [*sic*, penuche] was slightly liquefied but everything else ~~were~~ was perfect. No chrushed [*sic*] boxes or anything. Got a box of candy from Bella & John of the Bronx.

The grape jam was superb; (Et al) Christ <u>I'm well educated</u>. Jack Regan and I consumed both jars on crackers with eyes closed and concentrated on lovely visions of Conn., home, and stuff. Could you please send some more?[35]

The poignancy of this group of boys, so far from home, is summed up by Harry, "The favorite tune on the radio seems to be "I'm Dreaming of a (you know what)." It makes you feel pretty homesick hearing that, but of course you can't do much about it. Maybe I'll get home next Christmas."[36]

The *Snook* left on her disappointing eighth war patrol on Christmas Day 1944 and returned February 17, 1945. During this time spent patrolling off of the Kuril Islands, she only sighted two Soviet vessels and made no attacks on any enemy ships. At this point, the major submarine war was effectively over, and targets worthy of a torpedo were increasingly more difficult to acquire. Japanese merchant shipping, the primary prey of the submarine, had adopted the tactic of traveling, when possible, in the shallow waters along the coast to avoid the experienced and increasingly deadly American submarines. Submarines entering these areas would find better hunting but also more dangerous conditions, as the safety of the depths was farther away.

Harry signaled his return from the sea with a telegram on February 20, 1945, "Love to all the family. Am fit and well." He followed with a letter, with his characteristic critique of the quality and quantity of food during the patrol. He found that the chow, as usual, was good, but the variety, at times, only fair. "They steak and French fried us to death this run. It seemed as if every other meal was steak," he complained.[37] Previously content with an occasional beer, Harry shared with Mom and Pop his exploits with the beverage known as Gillie. Gillie, or torpedo juice, is derived from the alcohol fuel used to power the torpedo's steam engine. This fuel was denatured by the addition of a poison commonly known as "pink lady." The appropriately motivated *Snook* sailors had mastered the method of removing most of this additive by filtering the fuel through a compressed loaf of bread. Done incorrectly, the alcoholic spree could become deadly. Submarine veteran Warren Wildes related an incident that occurred on the *Flying Fish* before he reported onboard:

...they make this "gilly" they call it from torpedo alcohol and there was a process that they followed that they could really take the bad

132

stuff out of it. But I guess these guys got too far, they just ignored it and I think there were seven guys that ended up in the hospital. . . .Three or four of them died.... It's just poison. But some guys they were determined they were going to have their drinks."[38]

Harry took that chance too, apparently with no lasting ill effects, but wrote about some of the tolls exacted by the torpedo juice. "Love unrequited has not been robbing me of my rest but Gillie parties sure have. The boys of course need relaxation not saying a word about ulcers, heart burns and other symptoms which occur. Gillie is 180 proof you know."[39]

While Harry Julian's last two letters were upbeat, newsy, and positive, he was obviously beginning to tire of the conflict and looked forward to the time when he could return home. He was a skilled Torpedoman, a qualified submariner, and a veteran of three war patrols, but still just a hungry nineteen year old boy from Deep River, Connecticut. He was pleased that, "The jellie [sic] arrived in A1 condition and is resting in my locker right now waiting for an opportune time for its reopening. Thanks for it." He was less pleased that, "When all the ships (Jap) have been sunk I imagine they will find plenty to keep us busy. Shining brass, if nothing else. And God knows there is enough brass on this air conditioned sink drain." The last letter he wrote home contained a prescient and touching line; perhaps innocent enough, but considering the circumstance, quite poignant. He wrote, "Since this letter is my last for a long time it should be epic and history making and such, but since I don't feel very epic or anything it will have to be the same old line of stuff."[40]

The USS *Snook* left for her ninth and final war patrol on March 25, 1945, with the submarines USS *Burrfish* (SS 312) and *Bang* (SS 385), destined for the South China Sea and Luzon Strait. *Snook* detoured to Guam for emergency repairs, and when they were completed, headed toward her ordered rendezvous point. On station on April 8, she reported her position to the submarine USS *Tigrone* (SS 419) that was operating in the area as the leader of a Coordinated Attack Group consisting of four submarines, including *Snook*.[41] The *Tigrone* tried unsuccessfully to raise her on the radio the next day, but it was not until April 20, when the *Snook* failed to acknowledge a direction to rescue downed aviators, that her whereabouts was questioned. Failing to rendezvous with or respond to radio hails from the submarine *Bang*, she was classified as overdue and presumed lost on May 16.[42]

The fate of the *Snook* and location of her final mooring remain unknown. Harry did not return to Joanie, his parents, or the "oak clad hills" of Deep River. Harry and his shipmates, among them, Jack Regan, Warren Ellis, and Albert Gamberdella of Connecticut, Clarence "Ed" Edmunds of Knoxville, Tennessee, Chuck "Shaft Seven" Eckenrode of Altoona, Pennsylvania, and Victor Gregorini of Monongahela, Pennsylvania, all mentioned in his letters, remain on eternal patrol.

"... it's an honor to be a sub man."[43]

Harry F. Julian

Harry F. Julian and his three shipmates (23 December 1944). "The large one is of left to right Clarence Ed Edmunds of Knoxville, Tenn, Frenchy' Simonoeux [Simoneaux] from New Orleans, Chuck Shaft Seven Eckenrode of Altoona and of course me."[44]
Courtesy SFM

CHAPTER 10

ANALYSIS AND CONCLUSION

*How can we tell you there on land
what only the sub crews understand?
How can we say what the spirit means?
There is no death for submarines.*

Win Brooks, *Message From Submarine Overdue*

FIFTY-TWO SUBMARINES were lost during World War II. One out of every five boats that went on patrol never returned. Over 23 percent of the enlisted operational personnel, or 3,131 enlisted men, died while serving as crewmen on these submarines.[1] Duty on submarines was clearly understood to be dangerous duty; the navy even paid a 50 percent premium to those who would accept this hazardous assignment. Yet in spite of the danger, there was never a shortage of men to volunteer for submarine duty. Actually, due to the rigorous physical and mental standards one had to meet, it was more likely that a volunteer would be denied acceptance to the silent service than allowed acceptance into this elite group.

Personal comfort, hygiene, and entertainment conditions onboard a wartime submarine started at austere and moved rapidly towards appalling. Whether it was sharing a bunk with a shipmate or a torpedo, or eating and pursuing leisure-time activities with sixty other men in a mess hall the size of a child's bedroom, the space onboard allotted for the enlisted man gave the word "cramped" a whole new meaning. The showers, when they were not filled with potatoes, were generally secured. The submariner's ablutions were performed out of a bucket — that is, if the batteries, the diesel engines, and the Cook could spare the water. And that smell: a blend of unwashed human, engine exhaust, sanitary tank vents, and atomized oil. While the unique and pungent aroma probably defied precise analysis, once experienced, it undeniably shouted, submarine!

135

Submarines were dangerous for their crews; there was extremely little personal space and few crew comforts. They were hard on the physical and mental health of the men, and submarines smelled really awful. Yet, once having served on a submarine, men would do almost anything, including stowaway, to get back on.[2] Even with their impressive list of negative attributes, the submarine service consistently attracted a high caliber of volunteers and engendered a fierce loyalty in its veterans. The question remains as to what explains this apparent contradiction. What was it about the boats that caused men to turn their backs on safety, cleanliness, and comfort to ride beneath the waves?

For some, life aboard submarines was simply an acquired taste, and for the men who grew up in the towns of submarine builders and naval bases, that taste was developed early through close contact and familiarity. These men believed submarines were the only natural way to go to sea and to war. For example, prior to and during World War II, Electric Boat shipyard in Groton, Connecticut, employed local young men and their families to build, overhaul, and repair submarines. Many of these same men would go on to serve on the boats they helped build and learned to love.

However, propinquity cannot account for the entire population of submarine sailors' decision to volunteer. Many men, including four of the men interviewed for this book, began their careers in the surface navy and later migrated to submarines. Such a career path seems incongruous, since the life of an enlisted man on a battleship did have certain advantages. A number of what would be called "naval luxuries" on a sub were routine on a battleship. On a battleship, an enlisted man's clothes were stenciled and could be thrown in the department bag in the [berthing] compartment when dirty. The ship's laundry personnel would pick up, wash, and return them to the individual compartment, where a junior sailor was assigned to sort them and distribute them. Contrast this luxury to a fleet submarine at war where clothes, on the rare occasions when they were washed, would be laundered in a bucket by hand and only if a precious gallon of water could be spared. On the subs, bunks were shared, and personal storage space was microscopic, but on a battleship like the *Missouri* a typical berthing compartment housed thirty men in bunks stacked five high. Each man had his own bunk and his own locker for personal belongings. On a battleship, the ship's store was always open during the daytime, providing cigarettes, ice cream, "geedunk" (the navy term for candy), and other sundries. While crew recreation space was still limited to the berthing compartment, the mess hall, and the workspaces, the amount of free space available on most surface ships was vast compared to a fleet boat, so much so that movies were shown three times a week in the mess hall onboard the *Missouri* or, if it was nice weather out, the movie might be shown on the helicopter hanger deck, topside, at the aft end of the ship. On a fleet boat, movies were most often shown in the Forward Torpedo Room and competed with working Torpedomen and sleeping sailors for use of the space.

Given this relatively comfortable lifestyle, what drove men away from the surface ships? One characteristic that was objectionable to some was the fact that the routine on a surface ship was very formal and regimented. It was more like the "real" navy, especially on a battleship, where formality was at its highest level. While some men were attracted to the prestige, pageantry, and ritual of these premier capital ships, our sub sailors were not. Jackson Atkinson, another World War II submarine sailor who began his naval service in the surface fleet, complained about his time on the battleship *Maryland*, "...I couldn't even move without saluting somebody, or shining my shoes."[3] Robert Burr was more general about his dislike of surface ships when he said, "But I didn't like the destroyer and I didn't figure on getting anywhere at all."[4] Deen Brown probably summed it up best when he said, "One thing I liked about the submarine navy was, number one, it was not spit and polish regulation. Like [in] the battleship navy, sailors will spend half the day shining brightwork so the Captain's railings on his ladders would look good or something like that. That, to me, that was an awful waste of manpower."[5]

There was almost none of this spit-and-polish onboard a fleet submarine, with the possible exception of a little polishing of the torpedo tube doors. The close quarters, inability to routinely shower, and the generally hot and humid conditions, rendered such rituals pointless. Even the wearing of clothes and shaving were often set aside during a war patrol. As Atkinson related, "Everybody ran around with shorts and rags out of a rag bucket. You never saw anybody fully dressed."[6] It was also common to find submariners with a two month war-patrol beard, shaving before arrival in port. This informality, however, did not lead to anarchy, and although officers and enlisted men were much closer in their day-to-day interactions than would be the case on a naval surface ship, the chain of command and the respect due the officer's position remained intact. Atkinson confirmed this when he commented on the officer-enlisted relationships by stating, "I would say it was pretty close but I mean it was still 'mister'; the respect was still there."[7]

For the enlisted sailor in the surface fleet, there was also a clear disassociation from the crew as a whole. A man would know others in his department and might know men in an associated department, but most of the other sailors onboard would be strangers. There were areas of the ship where a Cook like Burr, for example, would never have gone. The engineering and weapons spaces would be a mystery. On a submarine however, a new crew member was required to quickly learn to draw every system, understand the functions of the routine and emergency equipment, and be able to perform the critical duties of every rating. Submarine qualification, along with the small size of the vessel, worked to weld the men into a unified crew. Sailors unable to qualify or judged discordant to the smooth operation of the boat were immediately removed. As was evident in these interviews and in discussions with almost all submariners, this unique and intimate connection with a single, cohesive unit was very attractive to the men.

One unexpected revelation was that the receipt of mail from home was not a morale-building attraction to all submariners. One might surmise that letters would be a strong motivational factor for sailors assigned to the far-roaming submarines, and for many, this was true. Certainly Harry Julian had a keen desire to both send and receive mail. Throughout his many months of correspondence, there are numerous instances of him goading, chiding, and encouraging the "home front" to respond to his letters more quickly, to send more letters, and to mail the occasional package of goodies. However, Robert Burr was of the opposite frame of mind; for him mail was of little interest. He explained "... but I wasn't one who wrote letters, so I didn't miss them, like a lot of people really missed the mail. Not that I didn't love my wife, it was just that I didn't have feelings that way, you know?"[8]

Aside from a natural disinclination, many men's apathy toward the mail was due to both the self-imposed and official naval censorship. An examination correspondence of the enlisted men during the war revealed an almost maddening adherence to the censor's order to discuss nothing of importance. Deen Brown elaborated, "About all you could say is, well, I'm okay, and here I am and...."[9] During the war, Paul Miller, the Chief of the Boat on the USS *Queenfish* (SS 393), was even more succinct. All that he ever wrote to his wife after a patrol was, "Safe but not sound. Well but not happy."[10]

The primary motivation for the prospective World War II submarine sailor was the opportunity to do something meaningful: to contribute to the American war effort in a tangible and measurable way. The fleet boat was on the frontline of the war in the Pacific. Rather than feel that in some oblique manner one's contribution mattered, the sub sailor knew that he had made a difference with every torpedo that detonated, with every ton of enemy shipping that went to the bottom, and with every Japanese transport that failed to reach its destination. Deen Brown echoed this feeling when he stated, "Submarine guys had something real to do. Meaningful. And that's what meant a lot to me; I wanted to do something meaningful and real. Never mind the spit and polish."[11] Brown's commanding officer, F.W. Fenno, seemed to agree when he noted in his second war patrol report that one of the greatest morale building tools was the sound of the detonation of your own torpedo on an enemy vessel.[12] Submarine sailors, unlike men in other parts of the service, received immediate feedback for their efforts.

Those in the navy charged with finding men for the boats during the war appeared to understand this desire to serve on the frontline and targeted it in many of their recruiting posters. Some of the captions on U.S. Navy submarine recruiting posters from World War II featured captions like, "See Action Now," "Train Today While You Fight For Tomorrow," and "Hit 'Em Where It Hurts – Join the Submarine Service," promising action in the frontline of the war. Although some of these types of posters targeted the men's desire for education or skill training, and certainly mentioned how, as a submariner, one obviously became more attractive to the opposite sex, the primary message was a summons to the men who wanted to make a difference, to be a fighting man, and to do something meaningful. This message on these posters was delivered in bold primary colors and rousing slogans. Images of sinking carriers, exploding ships, and burning enemy aircraft contained a "visual emphasis on the victorious outcome of a conflict at sea" and told the would-be submariner that his service would be productively spent on the front lines of the action. [13]

Men on submarine duty were paid a premium for their service on the boats, but this in and of itself was not a motivating factor for choosing or remaining in this hazardous duty. Certainly there was the understandable pleasure at receiving extra pay, but there was no indication that this was the deciding factor in anyone's decision to select such a dangerous occupation. Submarine pay was mentioned by almost all of the veterans, but only as a matter of fact. Even the 1943 edition of the *Bluejackets' Manual*, the navy recruit's handbook, details the amounts of pay and their occasions for their increase.[14] But while higher pay may have "baited the hook" of volunteering for the silent service, it apparently was not the deciding factor in their resolution to choose this dangerous occupation.

Danger lived with the men on the boats; they understood the hazards, faced them with what fortitude they had, and at times, experienced almost unendurable terror. The tales of men "peeing their pants" in fear are amusing to read, but demonstrated both the fear they felt, and their ability to remain at their posts even while so afraid that they lost bodily control. Part of this ability was the natural, and seemingly universal, perceived invincibility of these young men. In almost all of these interviews, the men confessed a lack of concern with their own death. As Dale Russell, shipmate of Warren Wildes, said in his book, *Hell Above, Deep Water Below*, "The thought of dying seldom crossed my mind; I was young and feeling invincible."[15] Another sub sailor, Donald B. Nobles, a Fire Control Technician on the USS *Aspro*, (SS 309), also exhibited this attitude in a letter to his sweetheart Grace when he bragged that he is "Tokyo's Nightmare."[16]

A tangible and submarine-specific mitigation to the fear of the danger of submarine duty was the understanding that it was an all or nothing bet; if a submariner came back from combat it would be in one piece, not crippled or disfigured as many of the army and surface navy veterans were. Robert Burr comforted his wife with the extraordinary rationale, "I said to my wife when we went to sea, I said, `If I get back, I'll be in one piece.' "[17] Originally an Aircraft Carrier sailor,

John Whitehead volunteered for submarine duty for the same reason. He said, "I didn't want to be beat up or badly wounded. I wanted to die quickly or come back home."[18] Obviously, for some, the prospect of returning "half-a-man" held more terror than that of not returning at all. In submarines during the war, there were very few instances of crew members being severely injured or disfigured in the line of duty. For boats and their crews fighting the Japanese in the dangerous environment of the sea, it was almost always all safe or all gone.

Vice Admiral Charles A. Lockwood was Commander Submarine Forces, Pacific Fleet, during the war. He summed up his appreciation of these special men who risked and lost their lives in the boats in his wartime memoirs:

> They were no supermen, nor were they endowed with any supernatural qualities of heroism. They were merely top-notch American lads, well trained, well treated, well armed and provided with superb ships. May God grant there will be no World War III; but, if there is, whether it be fought with the weapons we know or with weapons at whose type we can only guess, submarines and submariners will be in the thick of the combat, fighting with skill, determination and matchless daring for all of us and for our United States of America. [19]

The submarines took care of their men, sheltering them in their steel embrace like a protective mother. The boats took punishment from the enemy and experienced the pressure of depths far beyond what the designers and builders envisioned. But the subs demanded and received a price for this security; the total devotion of their men. The men gave it willingly and wore the embroidered dolphins on their sleeves as a sign of their membership in the undersea brotherhood. These submarine volunteers came from disparate locales like rural Georgia in the south and urban Connecticut in the north; from towns hugging the ocean's shore to landlocked states deep in the heartland. They came to find work, to avoid joining the family business, or to answer their country's call. They came straight to the boats, sought them later, or stumbled upon them. The men had many different secondary reasons for choosing submarines but one main reason; they wanted to do something meaningful.

NOTES:

Chapter 1
INTRODUCTION

1. Robert Hargis, *U.S. Submarine Crewman 1941-45* (Oxford: UK: Osprey Publishing, 2003), 11.
2. Theodore Roscoe, *United States Submarine Operations in World War II* (Annapolis, Maryland: United States Naval Institute, 1949), 493.

Chapter 2
THE LIFE SUBMARINE

1. Jacqueline S. Mitchell. "The Weight of the Water." *Scientific American Frontiers*, http://www.pbs.org/saf/1206/features/weight.htm.
2. Jeffery L. Rodengen, *The Legend of Electric Boat* (Ft. Lauderdale, Florida: Write Stuff Syndicate, 1994), 11. Note: Excerpted by the author from *La Vraie Histoire d'Alexandre*, a thirteenth century book.
3. Herbert S. Zim, *Submarines: The Story of Undersea Boats* (New York: Harcourt, Brace and Company, 1942), 10 - 12.
4. Clive Cussler and Craig Dirgo, *The Sea Hunters: True Adventures With Famous Shipwrecks* (NY: Simon and Schuster, 1996), 182; Jeffery L. Rodengen, *The Legend of Electric Boat* (Ft. Lauderdale, Florida: Write Stuff Syndicate, 1994), 15.
5. Rich Wills, former Assistant Underwater Archaeologist, Naval Historical Center, "*Hunley in Historical Context*" http://www.numa.net/articles/hunley_in_historical_context.html.
6. Grand Admiral von Tirpitz, *My Memoirs, Volumes I & II* (New York: Dodd, Mead and Company, 1919), 413.
7. Thomas D Parrish, *The Submarine: A History* (New York: Viking Penguin, 2004), 33.
8. Zim, *Submarines: The Story of Undersea Boats*, 46.
9. Ibid., 33 – 35; Robert Hatfield Barnes, *United States Submarines* (New Haven, Connecticut: H. F. Morse, 1946), 38 – 43.

10. Jane's Fighting Ships 1919 (New York: Arco Publishing, 1969. Originally published by London: Sampson Low Marston, 1919), 187; http://www.history.navy.mil/photos/sh-usn/usnsh-n/bb40.htm.

11. Barnes, *United States Submarines*, 206.

12. Bobette Gugliotta, *Pigboat 39* (Lexington, Kentucky: University Press of Kentucky, 1984), 98.

13. J. A Brillowski, "Sugar Boats Without Sugar," *Polaris Magazine*, June, 1996, 10.

14. Roscoe, *United States Submarine Operations in World War II*, 4.

15. Clay Blair, Jr., *Silent Victory: The U.S. Submarine War Against Japan* (New York: J. B. Lippincott, 1975), 27.

16. Flint Whitlock and Ron Smith. *The Depths of Courage: American Submariners at War with Japan, 1941 – 1945* (New York: Berkley Caliber, 2007), front piece.

17. Gary E. Weir, "The Search for an American Submarine Strategy and Design, 1919 – 1936" (*Naval War College Review* Volume XLIV, Number 1, Sequence 333, Winter 1991), 44.

18. United States Navy, *The Fleet Type Submarine – NAVPERS 16160* (Washington: US Government Printing Office, 1946), 6 - 16.

19. *The Bluejackets' Manual*. Ninth Edition. (Annapolis, Maryland: United States Naval Institute, 1939), 215 – 216.

20. Zim, *Submarines: The Story of Undersea Boats*, 68; Erminio Bagnasco, ed. *Submarines of World War Two*. (Annapolis, Maryland, Naval Institute Press, 1977), 212-213.

21. George Jones, ENC USN (ret.), interview by author, transcribed digital recording, East Lyme, Connecticut, 9 June 2009, 16.

22. John Deane, QMC USN (ret.), interview by author, digital recording, East Lyme, Connecticut, 28 May 2009.

23. Note: The Cross-section of American *Gato* Class Fleet Submarine can be used to follow the discussion these pages about the submarine internal compartments. This diagram was made using information from the book *The Fleet Type Submarine – NAVPERS 16160*, by examination of the *Gato* Class Submarine Cutaway Model at the U.S. Navy Submarine Force Museum (SFM), Groton, Connecticut, and by touring the USS *Lionfish* at Battleship Cove Museum, Fall River, Massachusetts.

24. United States Navy, *The Fleet Type Submarine – NAVPERS 16160*, 22 & Figure A-28; The *Gato* Class Submarine Cutaway Model (1:10 scale), SFM, Groton, Connecticut.

25. Martin Sheridan, *Overdue and Presumed Lost* (Annapolis, Maryland: Naval Institute Press, 2004; Originally published: Francestown, New Hampshire: M. Jones, 1947), 15. (page citations are to the reprint edition).

26. United States Navy, *The Fleet Type Submarine – NAVPERS 16160*, 28 & 29, 108.

27. Roscoe, *United States Submarine Operations in World War II*, 54.

28. John Field, "West to Japan," *LIFE Magazine*, March 15, 1943, 85.

29. Sheridan, *Overdue and Presumed Lost*, 41.

30. U.S.S. *Cod* WWII Submarine Memorial Committee. Photo Museum Guide. Oxford, Ohio: Oxford Museum Press, 1999, 64; Jim Christley, *U.S. Submarines 1941-45* (Oxford, UK: Osprey Publishing, 2006), 19; author's tour and measurement of the museum boat USS *Lionfish*, (SS 298) at Battleship Cove Museum, Fall River, Massachusetts.

31. Admiral Ignatius J. Galantin, USN (Ret.), *Take Her Deep: A Submarine Against Japan in World War II* (Chapel Hill, N.C: Algonquin Books of Chapel Hill, 1987), 54.

32. Christley, *U.S. Submarines 1941-45*, 6 & 8; Bagnasco, ed., *Submarines of World War Two*, 226.

33. Admiral Eugene B. Fluckey, *Thunder Below! The USS Barb Revolutionizes Submarine Warfare in World War II* (Chicago: University of Illinois Press, 1992), 15.

34. Dale Russell, *Hell Above Deep Water Below* (Seaside, Oregon: Frontier Publishing, 1995), 132.

35. Hargis, *U.S. Submarine Crewman 1941-45* (Oxford, UK: Osprey Publishing, 2003), 14.

36. Photographic Essay, "Submarine School: It Trains Men for Toughest Service," *LIFE Magazine*, 30 March 1942, 93.

37. Hargis, *U.S. Submarine Crewman 1941-45* (Oxford, UK: Osprey Publishing, 2003), 26 – 31.

38. Ibid., 26.

39. *Destination Tokyo*, dir. Delmer Daves. 135 min., Warner Bros. Pictures, 1943, Reissue Warner Home Video, 2004, DVD.

40. *The Bluejackets' Manual*. Eleventh Edition. (Annapolis, Maryland: United States Naval Institute, 1943), 1132 – 1133.

41. Hargis, *U.S. Submarine Crewman 1941-45*, 28 - 31.

42. *The Bluejackets' Manual*. Eleventh Edition, 1132.

43. Edward L. Beach, Commander, USN, *Submarine!* (New York, Henry Holt and Company, 1946), 5.

44. Russell, *Hell Above Deep Water Below*, 174 & 175.

45. Dudley "Mush" Morton, commanding, "USS *Wahoo* (SS238), Report of War Patrol Number Three." (Commander Submarine Force Pacific Fleet, 26 January 1943, typewritten and library bound, Book 238, SFL&M, Groton, Connecticut), 5.

46. Blair, *Silent Victory: The U.S. Submarine War Against Japan*, 357 – 358.

47. Beach, *Submarine!*, 159.

48. Ibid., 5.

49. *The Bluejackets' Manual*. Eleventh Edition., 137.

50. Charles W. Sasser and Craig Roberts, *One Shot - One Kill: American Combat Snipers, World War II, Korea, Vietnam, Beirut,* (New York: Pocket Star Books, 1990), 32 & 33.

51. Roscoe, *United States Submarine Operations in World War II*, 46, 253, & 527 – 563.

52. Blair, *Silent Victory: The U.S. Submarine War Against Japan*, 628, 630 – 631.

53. Ibid., 694 & 695.

54. *United States Submarine Losses – World War II*. Washington: U.S. Government Printing Office, 1946. Revised and reissued as NAVPERS 15,784 in 1949, 3.

55. Beach, *Submarine!*, 120.

56. R. D. Risser, commanding, "USS *Flying Fish* (SS 229), Report of War Patrol Number Eleven." (Commander Submarine Force Pacific Fleet, 22 October 1944, typewritten and library bound, Book 279, SFL&M, Groton, Connecticut), 68.

57. Photographic Essay, "U.S. Subs at Work," *LIFE Magazine*, 8 February 1943, 26.

Chapter 4
THE JACK-O'-THE-DUST:
Robert W. Burr, USS *Rasher* (SS 269)

1. *The Bluejackets' Manual*. Tenth Edition. (Annapolis, Maryland: United States Naval Institute, 1940), 421.
2. Robert W. Burr, CSC, USN (ret.), interview by author, transcribed digital recording, Uncasville, Connecticut, 21 March 2007, 2.
3. Ibid., 5.
4. Ibid., 6.
5. Ibid.,, 7 & 8.
6. Glenn A. Knoblock, *Black Submariners in the United States Navy, 1940 – 1975* (Jefferson, North Carolina: McFarland & Company, 2005), 56 & 57.
7. Robert W. Burr, interview by author, 21 March 2007, 10.
8. Note: Pratt & Whitney, located in central Connecticut, was and remains a world leader in the design, manufacture and service of aircraft engines and industrial gas turbines. http://www.pw.utc.com/.
9. Robert W. Burr, interview by author, 21 March 2007, 11.
10. Robert A. Heinlein, *Glory Road*, (New York: G. P. Putnam's Sons, 1963; New York: Orb Books, 2004), 26.
11. Robert W. Burr, interview by author, 21 March 2007, 13.
12. Ibid.
13. Ibid.
14. Ibid., 14.
15. Ibid., 18.
16. Note: The Manitowoc Shipbuilding Company produced twenty-eight submarines during World War II. These boats were "side-launched" due to the narrowness of the river at the shipyard. After construction the submarines were transported by barging them through the Chicago River, Chicago Sanitary and Ship Canal, Illinois River, and Mississippi River in a floating dry-dock. Final assembling was performed in New Orleans once the boats had cleared all canals and bridges.
17. Robert W. Burr, interview by author, 21 March 2007, 39.
18. Roscoe, *United States Submarine Operations in World War II*, 525.

19. Robert W. Burr, interview by author, 21 March 2007, 21.
20. E. S. Hutchinson, commanding, "USS *Rasher* (SS 269), Report of War Patrol Number One." (Commander Submarine Force Pacific Fleet, 24 November 1943, typewritten and library bound, Book 202, SFL&M, Groton, Connecticut), 8.
21. Robert W. Burr, interview by author, 21 March 2007, 21 & 22.
22. Ibid., 22.
23. Bagnasco, ed. *Submarines of World War Two*, 227.
24. Robert W. Burr, interview by author, 21 March 2007, 23.
25. Ibid., 37.
26. Ibid., 23.
27. Barnes, *United States Submarines*, 190 – 192.
28. Robert W. Burr, interview by author, 21 March 2007, 25.
29. Ibid., 25. 41.
30. Ibid., 37.
31. Ibid., 23.
32. E. S. Hutchinson, commanding, "USS *Rasher* (SS 269), Report of War Patrol Number One," 33.
33. Robert W. Burr, interview by author, 21 March 2007, 17.
34. Ibid., 27.
35. Ibid., 25.
36. Robert W. Burr, interview by author, 21 March 2007, 31.
37. Ibid.
38. Ibid., 17.
39. Ibid., 25.

Chapter 5
THE ARKANSAS PLOWBOY
George O. Jones, USS *Pogy* (SS 266)

1. George Jones, ENC, USN (ret.), interview by author, transcribed digital recording, East Lyme, Connecticut, 9 June 2009, 9.
2. Ibid., 5 & 6.
3. Ibid., 5.
4. Ibid., 9.
5. *Dictionary of American Naval Fighting Ships*, http://www.history.navy.mil/danfs/b9/bridge-i.htm.

6. Barbara W. Tuchman, *Stillwell and the American Experience in China, 1911 – 1945* (New York: MacMillan, 1970), 179.

7. George O. Jones, ENC SS USN RET. *Autobiography,* (Privately maintained at http://www.geocities.com/goliverjones/), Section 4 "Proud of Our Flag," 4.

8. George Jones, interview by author, 9 June 2009, 1.

9. Ibid., 10.

10. Ibid., 1 & 2.

11. *Dictionary of American Naval Fighting Ships,* http://www.history.navy.mil/danfs/s9/semmes-i.htm.

12. Ibid., http://www.history.navy.mil/danfs/f1/falcon-iii.htm.

13. George O. Jones, *Autobiography,* Section 6 "Blow and Vent College," 3.

14. *Dictionary of American Naval Fighting Ships,* http://www.history.navy.mil/danfs/m2/mallard-i.htm.

15. George Jones, interview by author, 9 June 2009, 14 & 15.

16. Ibid., 12 & 13.

17. Ibid., 14.

18. Ibid., 14.

19. George O. Jones, *Autobiography,* Section 21 "Route to Patrol Area," 3; Eddy, I. C., commanding, "USS *S-45* (SS156), Report of War Patrol Number One." (Commander Submarine Force Pacific Fleet, June 1942, typewritten and library bound; Book 156, SFL&M, Groton, Connecticut), 3.

20. George O. Jones, *Autobiography,* Section 22 "A Long Trip Home to Brisbane," 6.

21. Ibid., Section 23 "USS *S-38* My Next patrol," 2

22. Ibid., Section 23 "USS *S-38* My Next patrol," 3; Blair, *Silent Victory,* 274.

23. George Jones, interview by author, 9 June 2009, 18.

24. Munson, H. G. commanding, "USS *S-38* (SS143), Report of War Patrol Number Seven." (Commander Submarine Force Pacific Fleet, 2 September 1942, typewritten and library bound; Book 143, SFL&M, Groton, Connecticut), 12.

25. George Jones, interview by author, 9 June 2009, 18.

26. Ibid.

27. Ibid.,18 - 20; George O. Jones, *Autobiography,* Section 25 "Underway for my third patrol," 4

28. George Jones, interview by author, 9 June 2009, 18.
29. Note: Merthiolate Tincture is topical antiseptic solution composed of Benzalkonium Chloride, Alcohol, Acetone, Purified Water, and dye.
30. George Jones, interview by author, 9 June 2009, 21.
31. Note: The *S-38* would be officially credited in sinking only two enemy ships; the *Hayo Maru* on December 22, 1941 and the *Meiyo Maru* on August 8, 1942.
32. George Jones, interview by author, 9 June 2009, 22;
33. Wales, G. H. commanding, "USS *Pogy* (SS 266), Report of War Patrol Number Three." (Commander Submarine Force Pacific Fleet, 3 November 1943, typewritten and library bound; Book 266, SFL&M, Groton, Connecticut), 3.
34. George O. Jones, *Autobiography*, Section 29 "Submarine Base, Pearl Harbor, T. H.," 4.
35. Roscoe, *United States Submarine Operations in World War II*, 545; Metcalf, R. M. commanding, "USS *Pogy* (SS 266), Report of War Patrol Number Four." (Commander Submarine Force Pacific Fleet, 28 December 1943, typewritten and library bound; Book 266, SFL&M, Groton, Connecticut), 1 & 3.
36. Note: Post-war accounting did not confirm this sinking.
37. George Jones, interview by author, 9 June 2009, 24.
38. Note: Settings for depth, gyro angle, and speed were made by spindles that penetrated the tube and engaged their respective spindles in the torpedo. From, *21-Inch Submerged Torpedo Tubes*, Ordnance Pamphlet 1085, June 1944, found at http://www.maritime.org/fleetsub/tubes/chap8.htm
39. George Jones, interview by author, 9 June 2009, 24; Metcalf, R. M. commanding, "USS *Pogy* (SS 266), Report of War Patrol Number Four," 5 – 6.
40. George Jones, interview by author, 9 June 2009, 26.
41. Roscoe, *United States Submarine Operations in World War II*, 545; Metcalf, R. M. commanding, "USS *Pogy* (SS 266), Report of War Patrol Number Five." (Commander Submarine Force Pacific Fleet, 14 March 1944, typewritten and library bound; Book 266, SFL&M, Groton, Connecticut), 3.
42. George O. Jones, *Autobiography*, Section 32 "Hotel Gooney Bird," 4.

43. Metcalf, R. M. commanding, "USS *Pogy* (SS 266), Report of War Patrol Number Five," 3.
44. Roscoe, *United States Submarine Operations in World War II*, 545.
45. George Jones, interview by author, 9 June 2009, 28.
46. Ibid., 40.
47. Ibid., 30.
48. Ibid., 37.
49. Ibid., 39.
50. Ibid., 30.
51. Ibid.
52. Note: most likely Hiroshima, August 6, 1945; Nagasaki, August 9, 1945.
53. George Jones, interview by author, 9 June 2009, 32 & 33.
54. Ibid., 9.

Chapter 6

THE FAITHFUL SHIPMATE
Ernest "Ernie" V. Plantz, USS *Perch* (SS 176)

1. Ernie Plantz, EMC / Lt., USN, (ret.), interview by author, transcribed digital recording, Ledyard, Connecticut, 26 June 2009, 5.
2. Ibid., 9.
3. Ibid., 5.
4. Ibid., 6.
5. Ibid.
6. Ibid., 6.
7. Ibid., 10.
8. Ibid., 10.
9. Ibid., 14.
10. Roscoe, *United States Submarine Operations in World War II*, 29.
11. Ernie Plantz, interview by author, 26 June 2009, 14.
12. Ibid., 15.
13. *United States Submarine Losses – World War II*, 25.
14. Ernie Plantz, interview by author, 26 June 2009, 15.
15. *United States Submarine Losses – World War II*, 26.

16. Ernie Plantz, interview by author, 26 June 2009, 15.
17. Ibid., 15 & 16.
18. *United States Submarine Losses – World War II*, 26.
19. Ernie Plantz, interview by author, 26 June 2009, 42.
20. Ibid., 16.
21. Website concerning Dutch *Op ten Noort*-class hospital ships: http://www.netherlandsnavy.nl/Noort.htm.
22. Ernie Plantz, interview by author, 26 June 2009, 16.
23. Ibid., 41.
24. Ibid.
25. Ernie Plantz, interview by author, 26 June 2009, 16.
26. Ibid., 28.
27. Ibid.
28. Note: M. M. Turner, EM2; *United States Submarine Losses – World War II*, 27.
29. Ernie Plantz, interview by author, 26 June 2009, 28.
30. Ibid., 25.
31. Ibid., 19.
32. Ibid., 24.
33. Ibid., 23.
34. Ibid., 25 & 26.
35. Ibid., 24.
36. *United States Submarine Losses – World War II*, 27.
37. Ernie Plantz, interview by author, 26 June 2009, 24.
38. Ibid., 46.
39. Ibid., 19.
40. Ibid., 33.
41. Ibid., 20.
42. Ibid.
43. Ibid., 20.
44. Note: Sarmiento, M. CK1; *United States Submarine Losses – World War II*, 27.
45. Ernie Plantz, interview by author, 26 June 2009, 26.
46. Ibid., 27.
47. Ibid.
48. Ibid., 48.
49. Ibid., 31.
50. Ibid., 31.

51. Ibid., 34.
52. Ibid., 38.
53. Ibid., 44 & 45.
54. Ibid., 40.
55. Ibid., 30 & 40. Note: Caroline Plantz, Ernie's wife, also participated in this interview.
56. Ibid., 40.

Chapter 7

THE WILLING WARRIOR
Jeweldeen "Deen" Brown, USS *Trout* (SS 202)

1. Deen Brown, RMCM, USN, (ret.), interview by author, transcribed digital recording, Groton, Connecticut, 17 January
2007, 2.
2. Deen Brown, interview by author, 17 January 2007, 2.
3. Ibid., 5.
4. Ibid.
5. Ibid., 3.
6. Ibid., 6.
7. Ibid., 7.
8. Ibid.
9. Ibid., 7 & 8.
10. *Jane's Fighting Ships of WW II*. (London: Studio Editions Ltd.,
1989. Originally published by Jane's Publishing Co. 1946/47),
290 & 291.
11. F. W. Fenno, Jr., commanding, "USS *Trout* (SS 202), Report of
Second War Patrol." (Commander Submarine Force Pacific
Fleet, 6 March 1942, typewritten and library bound, Book 202,
U.S. Navy Submarine Force Museum, Groton, Connecticut), 2.
12. Blair, *Silent Victory: The U.S. Submarine War Against Japan*,
183 – 184.
13. Deen Brown, interview by author, 17 January 2007, 31.
14. Stowaway Holmes, The Eulogy of, from a copy of speaking
notes used by the U.S. Submarine Veterans of World War II –
Thames River Chapter.
15. Deen Brown, interview by author, 17 January 2007, 10.
16. Ibid., 36.

17. Blair, *Silent Victory: The U.S. Submarine War Against Japan*, 182, 190.

18. Deen Brown, interview by author, 17 January 2007, 14 & 15.

19. F. W. Fenno, Jr., commanding, "USS *Trout* (SS 202), Report of Third War Patrol." (Commander Submarine Force Pacific Fleet, 17 May 1942, typewritten and library bound, Book 202, SFL&M, Groton, Connecticut), 1.

20. F. W. Fenno, Jr., commanding, "USS *Trout* (SS 202), Report of Second War Patrol." 6.

21. Deen Brown, RMC, interview by author, 17 January 2007, 18 & 19.

22. Note: Excerpted from the author's copy of the article, given at the time of the interview.

23. Herbert A Werner, *Iron Coffins* (New York: Holt, Rinehart and Winston, 1969), 31.

24. Deen Brown, interview by author, 17 January 2007, 28 & 29.

25. F. W. Fenno, Jr., commanding, "USS *Trout* (SS 202), Report of Second War Patrol." 9.

26. Roscoe, *United States Submarine Operations in World War II*, 562.

27. Deen Brown, interview by author, 17 January 2007, 20.

28. Ibid.

29. Ibid., 21; L. P. Ramage, commanding, "USS *Trout* (SS 202), Report of Fifth War Patrol." (Commander Submarine Force Pacific Fleet, 13 October 1942, typewritten and library bound, Book 202, SFL&M, Groton, Connecticut), 4 - 7.

30. Note: This submarine was the former USS *Squalus* that sank during sea trials on May 23, 1939 in the waters off Portsmouth, NH. According to Brown, to be rescued by a previously "sunken" sub was a matter of some embarrassment for the sailors of the *Trout*.

31. *U.S. Submarine Losses: World War II*, 89; Blair, *Silent Victory: The U.S. Submarine War Against Japan*, 563 & 564.

32. Deen Brown, interview by author, 17 January 2007, 26.

33. Ibid., 30.

34. Ibid., 31.

35. Ibid., 35.

36. Ibid., 36.

Chapter 8
THE SELF-PROCLAIMED YOUNGSTER
Warren F. Wildes, USS *Flying Fish* (SS 229)

1. Warren F. Wildes, EM 3/c USN, interview by author, transcribed digital recording, Groton, Connecticut, 22 December 2006, 8.
2. Ibid., 7.
3. Blair, *Silent Victory: The U.S. Submarine War Against Japan*, 762 & 832; Darrell H. Zemitis, "Japanese Naval Transformation and the Battle of Tsushima," *Military Review (U.S. Army CGSC)* Volume: 84, Issue: 6 (November 1, 2004) Page: 73(3). Note: Not only was the Tsushima Strait an effective strategic barrier during World War II, it had been the stage for the decisive naval battle of the Russo-Japanese war in May of 1905. Using the natural tactical advantage of the narrow strait, the Japanese destroyed over two-thirds of the attacking Imperial Russian fleet, claimed the first defeat of a Western power by an Asian country, and established Japan as a major world naval power.
4. Warren F. Wildes, interview by author, 22 December 2006, 2.
5. Ibid., 3.
6. Ibid., 4.
7. Blair, *Silent Victory: The U.S. Submarine War Against Japan*, 838.
8. Russell, *Hell Above Deep Water Below*, 160.
9. *United States Submarine Losses – World War II*, 67 - 70.
10. Warren F. Wildes, interview by author, 22 December 2006, 4.
11. R. D. Risser, commanding, "USS *Flying Fish* (SS 229), Report of War Patrol Number Twelve." (Commander Submarine Force Pacific Fleet, 4 July 1945, typewritten and library bound, Book 279, U.S. Navy Submarine Force Museum, Groton, Connecticut), 8.
12. Warren F. Wildes, interview by author, 22 December 2006, 9; Scrapbook *Flying Fish* Book SS 229, (SFL&M, Groton, Connecticut), POW Letter.
13. R. D. Risser, commanding, "USS *Flying Fish* (SS 229), Report of War Patrol Number Twelve." 9.
14. Russell, *Hell Above Deep Water Below*, 132.

15. Warren F. Wildes, interview by author, 22 December 2006, 22.

16. Scrapbook USS *Flying Fish* Book SS 229, POW Letter.

17. Warren F. Wildes, interview by author, 22 December 2006, 21.

18. Russell, *Hell Above Deep Water Below*, 131.

19. Warren F. Wildes, interview by author, 22 December 2006, 13.

20. Ibid., 12.

21. Ibid., 11.

22. Ibid., 1 & 2.

23. Pierce, G. E. commanding, "USS *Tunny* (SS282), Report of War Patrol Number Nine." (Commander Submarine Force Pacific Fleet, 15 September 1945, typewritten and library bound; Book 282, SFL&M, Groton, Connecticut), 15.

24. Blair, *Silent Victory: The U.S. Submarine War Against Japan*, 838 & 839.

25. Sheridan, *Overdue and Presumed Lost*, v; *United States Submarine Losses – World War II*, 15.

26. Blair, *Silent Victory: The U.S. Submarine War Against Japan*, 839.

27. Warren F. Wildes, interview by author, 22 December 2006, 11.

28. Ibid., 8.

29. Ibid., 14.

30. Russell, *Hell Above Deep Water Below*, 178.

31. Warren F. Wildes, interview by author, 22 December 2006, 14.

32. Ibid., 14.

33. Ibid., 14 & 15.

34. Ibid., 21.

35. Ibid., 16 & 17.

36. Ibid., 8.

Chapter 9
THE ABSENT COMPANION
Harry F. Julian, USS *Snook* (SS 279)

1. Harry F. Julian, TM 3/c, USN, transcription, letter to mother, Deep River, Connecticut, Sat. July 3, 1943, transcribed by author, The Harry Julian Papers, Collection of Letters and Clippings, Accession Number: NM 94.74, SFL&M, Naval Submarine Base New London, Groton, Connecticut 06349-5571.

Note: This collection of letters in its entirety was transcribed by the author from the original documents. Where possible slang, strikethroughs, shorthand, and other manuscript idiosyncrasies were preserved. Only to remove confusion for the reader was the term [*sic*] used within the sections quoted from Harry's letters to indicate "as originally written."

2. Harry F. Julian, letter to sister, Deep River, Connecticut, Sat. July 9, 1943.

3. Harry F. Julian, letter to mother, Sat. Aug 29, 1943.

4. Harry F. Julian, letter to mother, Sat. Aug 29, 1943.

5. Harry F. Julian, letter to mother, dates July 15, 1943, July 30, 1943, Aug 6, 1943, Aug 31, 1943, & Sept. 1, 1943.

6. Harry F. Julian, letter to mother, July 27, 1943.

7. Harry F. Julian, letter to mother, Sept. 5, 1943.

8. Harry F. Julian, letter to mother, Sept. 9, 1943.

9. Harry F. Julian, letter to mother, Sept. 17, 1943.

10. Harry F. Julian, letter to mother, March 27, 1944.

11. Harry F. Julian, letter to mother, Apr 9, 1944.

12. Harry F. Julian, letter to mother, April 29, 1944.

13. Harry F. Julian, letter to mother, May 2, 1944.

14. Harry F. Julian, letter to sister and family, Deep River, Connecticut, May 9, 1944.

15. Harry F. Julian, letter to mother and father, Deep River, Connecticut, May 19, 1944.

16. *United States Submarine Losses – World War II*, 161; Roscoe, *United States Submarine Operations in World War II*, 555.

17. Harry F. Julian, letter to Barbara, Deep River, Connecticut, May 20, 1944.

18. Harry F. Julian, letter to mother and father, May 20, 1944.

19. Harry F. Julian, letter to mother and father, May 30, 1944.

20. Harry F. Julian, letter to mother and father, Jun 11, 1944.

21. G. H. Browne, commanding, "USS *Snook* (SS279), Report of War Patrol Number Six." (Commander Submarine Force Pacific Fleet, 15 August 1944, typewritten and library bound, Book 279, SFL&M, Groton, Connecticut), 1.

22. Harry F. Julian, letter to mother and father, Jun 24, 1944.

23. Harry F. Julian, letter to mother and father, Aug 14, 1944.

24. Harry F. Julian, letter to mother and father, Aug 31, 1944.

25. G. H. Browne, commanding, "USS *Snook* (SS 279), Report of War Patrol Number Seven." (Commander Submarine Force Pacific Fleet, 18 November 1944, typewritten and library bound, Book 279, SFL&M, Groton, Connecticut), 3.
26. Harry F. Julian, letter to mother and father, Sept 24, 1944.
27. Roscoe, *United States Submarine Operations in World War II*, 555; Lee A. Gladwin, "American POWs on Japanese Ships Take a Voyage into Hell," *Prologue Magazine* Vol. 35, No. 4 (Winter 2003) : http://www.archives.gov/publications/prologue/2003/winter/hell-ships-1.html.
28. Harry F. Julian, letter to mother and father, Nov 14, 1944.
29. Ibid.
30. Harry F. Julian, letter to mother and father, May 8, 1944 & May 11, 1944.
31. Note: This was John B. Regan, Fireman First Class, lost on the *Snook. United States Submarine Losses – World War II*, 163.
32. Harry F. Julian, letter to mother and father, Dec. 9 & 22, 1944; Note: "Ferdinands" most likely refers to the flower-smelling bull in the Munro Leaf children's book, The Story of *Ferdinand* (1936) that was made into a Disney short animated film entitled *Ferdinand the Bull* in 1938.
33. Note: This was McNeill, D. J. LTJG, lost on the *Snook. United States Submarine Losses – World War II*, 163.
34. Harry F. Julian, letter to mother and father, Dec 18 1944.
35. Harry F. Julian, letter to mother and father, Dec 23 1944.
36. Harry F. Julian, letter to mother and father, Dec 22 1944.
37. Harry F. Julian, letter to mother and father, Feb 16 & 20, 1945.
38. Warren F. Wildes, interview by author, 22 December 2006, 16.
39. Harry F. Julian, letter to mother and father, Feb 23 1944 [5].
40. Harry F. Julian, letter to mother and father, March 22 1945.
41. Cassedy, H., commanding, "USS *Tigrone* (SS419), Report of War Patrol Number One." Commander Submarine Force Pacific Fleet, 5 May 1945, typewritten and library bound; Book 419, SFL&M, Groton, Connecticut, 29.
42. *United States Submarine Losses – World War II*, 161.
43. Harry F. Julian, letter to mother, Aug 29, 1943.
44. Harry F. Julian, letter to mother, December 23, 1944.

Chapter 10
ANALYSIS AND CONCLUSION

1. Roscoe, *United States Submarine Operations in World War II*, 493.

2. Stowaway Holmes, *The Eulogy of*, from a copy of speaking notes used by the U.S. Submarine Veterans of World War II – Thames River Chapter.

3. Jackson C. Atkinson Jr., Chief Engineman USN (ret.). interview by author, 16 February 2007 at SubVets, Groton, 2.

4. Robert W. Burr, interview by author, 21 March 2007, 9.

5. Deen Brown, interview by author, 17 January 2007, 36.

6. Jackson C. Atkinson Jr., interview by author, 16 February 2007, 4.

7. Ibid., 13.

8. Robert W. Burr, interview by author, 21 March 2007, 31.

9. Deen Brown, interview by author, 17 January 2007, 30.

10. Paul Miller stories:
   http://www.queenfish.org/noframes/stories2.html

11. Deen Brown, interview by author, 17 January 2007, 36.

12. F. W. Fenno, Jr., commanding, "USS *Trout* (SS202), Report of War Patrol Number Two," 9.

13. Then and Now,
   http://www.navy.mil/navydata/cno/n87/usw/issue_13/now_then.html

14. *The Bluejackets' Manual*. Eleventh Edition. 1132.

15. Russell, *Hell Above Deep Water Below*, 88.

16. Donald B Nobles, FCS 3/c, USN, letter to Grace, Los Angeles, California, December 4, 1942, Collection of Letters, Personal Collection of the Author, East Lyme, Connecticut.

17. Robert W. Burr, interview by author, 21 March 2007, 25.

18. Knoblock, *Black Submariners in the United States Navy, 1940 – 1975*, 42.

19. Vice Admiral Charles A. Lockwood, Jr., *"Sink 'Em All"* (New York: Dutton, 1951), 125.

SELECTED BIBLIOGRAPHY

PRIMARY SOURCES

Books

Beach, Edward L. *Submarine!* New York: Henry Holt and Company, 1946.

Conner, Claude C. *Nothing Friendly in the Vicinity.* Annapolis, Maryland, Naval Institute Press, 2004. Originally published: Mason City, Iowa: Savas, 1999.

Fluckey, Admiral Eugene B. *Thunder Below! The USS Barb Revolutionizes Submarine Warfare in World War II.* Chicago: University of Illinois Press, 1992.

Galantin, Admiral Ignatius J., USN (Ret.). *Take Her Deep: A Submarine Against Japan in World War II.* Chapel Hill, N.C: Algonquin Books of Chapel Hill, 1987.

Jane's Fighting Ships 1919. New York: Arco Publishing, 1969. Originally published by London: Sampson Low Marston, 1919.

Jane's Fighting Ships of WW II. London: Studio Editions Ltd., 1989. Originally published by Jane's Publishing Co. 1946/47.

Keith, Don. *In the Course of Duty.* New York: New American Library / Penguin, 2005.

Russell, Dale. *Hell Above, Deep Water Below.* Tillamook, Oregon: Bayocean Enterprises, 1995.

von Tirpitz, Grand Admiral. *My Memoirs, Volumes I & II.* New York: Dodd, Mead and Company, 1919.

Werner, Herbert A. *Iron Coffins.* New York: Holt. Rinehart and Winston, 1969.

Military Publications

21-Inch Submerged Torpedo Tubes, Ordnance Pamphlet 1085, June 1944, http://www.maritime.org/fleetsub/tubes/chap8.htm.

United States Navy. *The Fleet Type Submarine – NAVPERS 16160*. Washington: US Government Printing Office, 1946, reprint by www.periscopefilm.com.

The Bluejackets' Manual. Ninth Edition. Annapolis, Maryland, United States Naval Institute, 1939.

The Bluejackets' Manual. Tenth Edition. Annapolis, Maryland, United States Naval Institute, 1940.

The Bluejackets' Manual. Eleventh Edition. Annapolis, Maryland, United States Naval Institute, 1943.

United States Submarine Losses – World War II. Washington: U.S. Government Printing Office, 1946. Revised and reissued as NAVPERS 15,784 in 1949.

Magazines, Articles, and Journals

Brillowski, J. A. "Sugar Boats Without Sugar." *Polaris Magazine*, June, 1996, 10.

Collections

Julian, Harry F. The Harry Julian Papers, Collection of Letters and Clippings, Accession Number: NM 94.74, U.S. Navy Submarine Force Museum, Naval Submarine Base New London, Groton, Connecticut.

Nobles, Donald B. Collection of Letters, Personal Collection of the Author, East Lyme, Connecticut.

A collection of the letters from this sailor to his friend, girlfriend, fiancé, and finally wife, Grace. Nobles was a Fire Control Technician Third Class and served on the USS *Aspro* (SS 309), The USS *Pipefish* (SS 388), and as a member of a relief crew in Submarine Divisions 44 and 122.

Interviews by the Author

Atkinson, Jackson C. Jr., Chief Engineman USN (ret.). Interview by author, 16 February 2007, at SubVets, Groton, Connecticut. Digital recording– transcribed.

Engineman on USS *Sturgeon* for seven war patrols.

Brown, Jeweldeen "Deen," Master Chief Radioman USN (ret.). Interview by author, 17 January 2007, Montville, Connecticut. Digital recording – transcribed.

Radioman on USS *Trout* for eight war patrols.

Burr, Robert W., Chief Commissary Steward USN (ret.). Interview by author, 21 March 2007, Uncasville, Connecticut. Digital recording – transcribed.

Commissary Steward on USS *Rasher* for two war patrols and USS *Redfin* for two war patrols

Deane, John, Chief Quartermaster USN (ret.). Interview by author, 28 May 2009, East Lyme, Connecticut, Digital recording.

Quartermaster on USS *Bluegill* (SS 242) for pre-commissioning detail and three war patrols, USS *S-47* for two war missions.

Grills, Richard A., Teleman Third Class, USN. Interview by author, 21 August 2008, Ashaway, Rhode Island. Digital recording.

Communications Clerk on USS *Missouri* (BB 63), 1952 – 1953.

Jones, George O., Chief Engineman USN (ret.). Interview by author, 9 June 2009, East Lyme, Connecticut, Digital recording– transcribed.

Engineman on USS *S-45* for one war patrol, USS *S-38* for two war patrols, and USS *Pogy* for four war patrols.

Metzger, Richard, Officer, Interview by author, 21 March 2007, Uncasville, Connecticut, Digital recording.

Officer on USS *Hake* for seven war patrols

Plantz, Ernie, Chief Electrician's Mate / Lieutenant, USN. Interview by author, 26 June 2009, Ledyard, Connecticut. Digital recording – transcribed.

Electrician's Mate on USS *Perch* on two war patrols before the ship's scuttling. Spent 1,297 days in a Japanese POW camp until his release at war's end.

Wildes, Warren F., Electrician's Mate Third Class. USN. Interview by author, 22 December 2006, Groton, Connecticut. Digital recording – transcribed.

Electrician's Mate on USS *Flying Fish* on their final war patrol before war's end.

Scrapbooks

These "Boat Books" scrapbooks are located at the U.S. Navy Submarine Force Museum, Naval Submarine Base, Groton, Connecticut. They contain miscellaneous articles, notes, personal and official U.S. Navy photographs, and other items related to specific submarines.

USS *Flying Fish* (SS 229)

USS *Perch* (SS 176)

USS *Pogy* (SS 266)

USS *Rasher* (SS 269)

USS *Redfin* (SS 272)

USS *S-16* (SS 121)

USS *S-24* (SS 129)

USS *S-38* (SS143)

USS *S-45* (SS156)

USS *S-48* (SS 159)

USS *Snook*, (SS 279)

USS *Sturgeon* (SS 187)

USS *Trout* (SS 202)

USS *Wahoo* (SS 238)

War Patrol Reports: United States Navy. Reports of Submarine War Patrols.

Library bound War Patrol Reports are available for every World War II submarine. These books are archived at the U.S. Navy Submarine Force Museum, Groton, Connecticut and contain the archived official post-patrol report for each submarine.

Browne, G. H., commanding, "USS *Snook* (SS 279), Report of War Patrol Number Six." Commander Submarine Force Pacific Fleet, 15 August 1944, typewritten and library bound; Book 279, U.S. Navy Submarine Force Museum, Groton, Connecticut.

Browne, G. H., commanding, "USS *Snook* (SS 279), Report of War Patrol Number Seven." Commander Submarine Force Pacific Fleet, 18 November 1944, typewritten and library bound; Book 279, U.S. Navy Submarine Force Museum, Groton, Connecticut.

Cassedy, H., commanding, "USS *Tigrone* (SS 419), Report of War Patrol Number One." Commander Submarine Force Pacific Fleet, 5 May 1945, typewritten and library bound; Book 419, U.S. Navy Submarine Force Museum, Groton, Connecticut.

Eddy, I. C., commanding, "USS *S-45* (SS 156), Report of War Patrol Number One." Commander Submarine Force Pacific Fleet, June 1942, typewritten and library bound; Book 156, U.S. Navy Submarine Force Museum, Groton, Connecticut.

English, R. H. commanding, "USS *S-38* (SS 143), Report of War Patrol Number Eight." Commander Submarine Force Pacific Fleet, 29 October 1942, typewritten and library bound; Book 143, U.S. Navy Submarine Force Museum, Groton, Connecticut.

Fenno, F. W., Jr., commanding, "USS *Trout* (SS 202), Report of War Patrol Number Two." Commander Submarine Force Pacific Fleet, 6 March 1942, typewritten and library bound; Book 202, U.S. Navy Submarine Force Museum, Groton, Connecticut.

Fenno, F. W., Jr., commanding, "USS *Trout* (SS 202), Report of War Patrol Number Three." Commander Submarine Force Pacific Fleet, 17 May 1942, typewritten and library bound; Book 202, U.S. Navy Submarine Force Museum, Groton, Connecticut.

Hutchinson, E. S., commanding, "USS *Rasher* (SS 269), Report of War Patrol Number One." Commander Submarine Force Pacific Fleet, 24 November 1943, typewritten and library bound; Book 269, U.S. Navy Submarine Force Museum, Groton, Connecticut.

Metcalf, R. M. commanding, "USS *Pogy* (SS 266), Report of War Patrol Number Four." Commander Submarine Force Pacific Fleet, 28 December 1943, typewritten and library bound; Book 266, U.S. Navy Submarine Force Museum, Groton, Connecticut.

Metcalf, R. M. commanding, "USS *Pogy* (SS 266), Report of War Patrol Number Five." Commander Submarine Force Pacific Fleet, 14 March 1944, typewritten and library bound; Book 266, U.S. Navy Submarine Force Museum, Groton, Connecticut.

Metcalf, R. M. commanding, "USS *Pogy* (SS 266), Report of War Patrol Number Six." Commander Submarine Force Pacific Fleet, 8 June 1944, typewritten and library bound; Book 266, U.S. Navy Submarine Force Museum, Groton, Connecticut.

Morton, Dudley "Mush" commanding, "USS *Wahoo* (SS 238), Report of War Patrol Number Three." Commander Submarine Force Pacific Fleet, 26 January 1943, typewritten and library bound; Book 238, U.S. Navy Submarine Force Museum, Groton, Connecticut.

Munson, H. G. commanding, "USS *S-38* (SS 143), Report of War Patrol Number Seven." Commander Submarine Force Pacific Fleet, 2 September 1942, typewritten and library bound; Book 143, U.S. Navy Submarine Force Museum, Groton, Connecticut.

Pierce, G. E. commanding, "USS *Tunny* (SS 282), Report of War Patrol Number Nine." Commander Submarine Force Pacific Fleet, 15 September 1945, typewritten and library bound; Book 282, U.S. Navy Submarine Force Museum, Groton, Connecticut.

Ramage, L. P., commanding, "USS *Trout* (SS 202), Report of Fifth War Patrol." Commander Submarine Force Pacific Fleet, 13 October 1942, typewritten and library bound; Book 202, U.S. Navy Submarine Force Museum, Groton, Connecticut.

Risser, R. D. commanding, "USS *Flying Fish* (SS 229), Report of War Patrol Number Eleven." Commander Submarine Force Pacific Fleet, 22 October 1944, typewritten and library bound; Book 229, U.S. Navy Submarine Force Museum, Groton, Connecticut.

Risser, R. D. commanding, "USS *Flying Fish* (SS 229), Report of War Patrol Number Twelve." Commander Submarine Force Pacific Fleet, 4 July 1945, typewritten and library bound; Book 229, U.S. Navy Submarine Force Museum, Groton, Connecticut.

Wales, G. H. commanding, "USS *Pogy* (SS 266), Report of War Patrol Number Three." Commander Submarine Force Pacific Fleet, 3 November 1943, typewritten and library bound; Book 266, U.S. Navy Submarine Force Museum, Groton, Connecticut.

SECONDARY SOURCES

Books

Bagnasco, Erminio, ed. *Submarines of World War Two*. Annapolis, Maryland, Naval Institute Press, 1977.

Barnes, Robert Hatfield. *United States Submarines*. New Haven, Connecticut: H. F. Morse, 1946.

Blair, Clay Jr. *Silent Victory: The U.S. Submarine War Against Japan*. New York: J. B. Lippincott, 1975.

Christley, Jim. *U.S. Submarines 1941-45*. Oxford, UK: Osprey Publishing, 2006.

Cussler, Clive and Craig Dirgo. *The Sea Hunters: True Adventures With Famous Shipwreck*. NY: Simon and Schuster, 1996.

Gugliotta, Bobette. *Pigboat 39*. Lexington, Kentucky: University Press of Kentucky, 1984.

Hargis, Robert. *U.S. Submarine Crewman 1941-45*. Oxford, UK: Osprey Publishing, 2003.

Hoyt, Edwin P. *Submarines At War: The History of the American Silent Service*. Brancliff Manor, NY: Stein and Day, 1983.

Knoblock, Glenn A. *Black Submariners in the United States Navy, 1940 – 1975*. Jefferson, North Carolina: McFarland & Company, 2005.

Newpower, Anthony. *Iron Men and Tin Fish*. Westport, Connecticut, Praeger Security / Greenwood, 2006.

Parrish, Thomas. *The Submarine: A History*. New York: Viking/Penguin, 2004.

Rodengen, Jeffery L., *The Legend of Electric Boat*. Ft. Lauderdale, Florida: Write Stuff Syndicate, 1994.

Roscoe, Theodore. *United States Submarine Operations in World War II*. Annapolis, Maryland: United States Naval Institute, 1949.

Sasser, Charles W. and Craig Roberts. *One Shot - One Kill: American Combat Snipers, World War II, Korea, Vietnam, Beirut*. New York: Pocket Star Books, 1990.

Sheridan, Martin. *Overdue and Presumed Lost*. Francestown, New Hampshire: M. Jones, 1947, reprint by Annapolis, Maryland: Naval Institute Press, 2004.

Tuchman, Barbara W. *Stillwell and the American Experience in China, 1911 – 1945*. New York: MacMillan, 1970.

U.S.S. *Cod* WWII Submarine Memorial Committee. *Photo Museum Guide*. Oxford, Ohio: Oxford Museum Press, 1999.

Whitlock, Flint and Ron Smith. *The Depths of Courage: American Submariners at War with Japan, 1941 – 1945*. New York: Berkley Caliber, 2007.

Zim, Herbert S. *Submarines: The Story of Undersea Boats*. New York: Harcourt, Brace and Co., 1942.

Magazines, Articles, Journals, and Other Sources

Destination Tokyo. Directed by Delmer Daves. 135 min. Warner Bros. Pictures, 1943. Reissue Warner Home Video, 2004. DVD.

Field, John. "West to Japan." *LIFE Magazine*, March 15, 1943, 84 - 96.

Gladwin, Lee A. "American POWs on Japanese Ships Take a Voyage into Hell," *Prologue Magazine,* Vol. 35, No. 4 (Winter 2003): http://www.archives.gov/publications/prologue/2003/winter/hell-ships-1.html.

Mitchell, Jacqueline S. "The Weight of the Water." *Scientific American Frontiers,* http://www.pbs.org/saf/1206/features/weight.htm

Photographic Essay. "Submarine School: It Trains Men for Toughest Service." *LIFE Magazine,* 30 March 1942, 93 - 101.

Photographic Essay. "U.S. Subs at Work." *LIFE Magazine,* 8 February 1943, 26 - 27.

Stowaway Holmes. *The Eulogy of,* from a copy of speaking notes used by the U.S. Submarine Veterans of World War II – Thames River Chapter.

Weir, Gary E. "The Search for an American Submarine Strategy and Design, 1919 – 1936." *Naval War College Review* Volume XLIV, Number 1, Sequence 333 (Winter 1991), 34 – 46.

Wills, Rich, former Assistant Underwater Archaeologist, Naval Historical Center. "Hunley in Historical Context" http://www.numa.net/articles/hunley_in_historical_context.html.

Zemitis, Darrell H. "Japanese Naval Transformation and the Battle of Tsushima." *Military Review (U.S. Army CGSC)* Volume: 84, Issue: 6 (November 1, 2004).

Submarine-Related Websites

http://www.archives.gov/publications/prologue/2003/winter/hell-ships-1.html

The internet site of the Nation Archives.

http://www.battleshipcove.org/ss298-history.htm

The Internet site of Battleship Cove, home of the World War II fleet boat USS *Lionfish*, (SS 298).

http://www.history.navy.mil/danfs.

Dictionary of American Naval Fighting Ships maintained by the Naval History & Heritage Command (SH), Washington Navy Yard, 805 Kidder Breese Street SE, Washington Navy Yard, DC 20374-5060

http://www.geocities.com/goliverjones/

Domain page for George O. Jones. ENC SS USN RET. *"Autobiography."* Privately maintained.

http://www.navy.mil/navydata/cno/n87/usw/issue_13/now_then.html

The Internet site of the Naval Historical Center, an official U.S. Navy web site.

http://www.ussnautilus.org/

The Internet site of the Historic Ship Nautilus and U.S. Navy Submarine Force Museum, Groton, Connecticut.

General Note:

All notes, references, and cited sources were accurate as of January 16, 2010. All websites referenced were also confirmed active and relevant as of January 16, 2010.

INDEX